VOLKER WEIDERMANN

DREAMERS

WHEN THE WRITERS TOOK POWER, GERMANY, 1918

TRANSLATED FROM THE GERMAN BY RUTH MARTIN

PUSHKIN PRESS

Pushkin Press
71–75 Shelton Street
London WC2H 9JQ

Original text © 2017 Volker Weidermann
English translation © 2018 Ruth Martin
Copyright © Verlag Kiepenheuser & Witsch

Dreamers was first published as *Träumer* in Germany, 2017
First published by Pushkin Press in 2018

GOETHE
INSTITUT

The translation of this work was supported by a grant from the
Goethe-Institut

9 8 7 6 5 4 3 2 1

ISBN 13: 978-1-78227-504-6

Translation of *To Hedwig Zapf* by Marielle Sutherland

Every effort has been made to trace the copyright holders and obtain permission
to reproduce the quoted material from Oskar Maria Graf's "Adage". Please do
get in touch with any enquiries or any information relating to the rights holder.

Designed and typeset by Tetragon, London
Printed and bound by CPI Group (UK) Ltd, Croydon, CRO 4YY

www.pushkinpress.com

DREAMERS

DREAMERS

THE SHOT

IT HAD BEEN A FAIRY TALE, of course—nothing but a fairy tale that had become reality for a few weeks. And now it was over. It would have been ridiculous to cling to power any longer: the election results in January had been too devastating for that. Two per cent, it was a joke, a cruel, bad joke. Ever since, the press had been subjecting him not only to more of their frenzied hatred, but to mockery and scorn as well. A people's king without a people, a jester on the king's throne, un-Bavarian crackpot, Jewish upstart.

Kurt Eisner had given up. His negotiations with his archenemy Erhard Auer, the leader of the Social Democrats, had gone on late into the night. "Negotiations" was hardly the right word. He had nothing left to bargain with. Auer had offered him the position of Ambassador to Prague; he might as well have said Consular Secretary to Australia. It was over. He'd had his chance and done what he could to transform the Kingdom of Bavaria into a people's republic, a land of solidarity and altruism.

It was a dream, to suddenly find himself sitting in the prime minister's seat on the night of 7th November. Sometimes you just had to be quick-witted enough to recognize the moment when it arrived. And it arrived on 7th November 1918.

A sunny afternoon; tens of thousands of soldiers, sailors, unionists and workers had gathered on the western slope of the Theresienwiese. The mood was tense. The Minister of the Interior, von Brettreich, had had the city plastered with posters announcing that order would be maintained. The Social Democratic Party's Erhard Auer had given him his personal assurance of that the previous day. A revolution was not about to break out. Kurt Eisner, parliamentary candidate for the Independent Social Democrats, who had been invoking the coming revolution for days, would be "forced to the wall", that was how Auer had put it. He said he had the situation in hand.

He didn't have anything in hand. There was chaos that afternoon: more and more people arriving; soldiers streaming in from the barracks, most of them having torn off their insignia. The men—and a few women—stood in little groups, clustering first around one speaker, then another. Auer had secured the best position for himself, on the grand steps leading up to the statue of Bavaria. But when the crowds realized he was just trying to placate them, promising them jam in some far-off tomorrow, they moved on to the other speakers further down the slope.

Kurt Eisner was standing right at the bottom. He was almost yelling, waving his arms in the air. A crowd was forming around the man with the long grey hair, the pince-nez, the wild beard and the large hat. He had a good name among those who were hoping for revolution: he had organized the munition workers' strike in January, had spent six months in prison for it.

His speaking style was not particularly rousing; his voice was scratchy and high-pitched. He had some trouble making himself heard above the other speakers. But the crowd sensed that, today, this was their man. He wasn't going to send them home. He could feel the energy of the day, the rage, the will for some decisive thing to happen at last. The king had been seen that morning taking a stroll through the English Garden. Well, how much longer did he want to go on strolling? How much longer did he want to rule?

A young radical pacifist in a black coat—a coarse-featured baker's son from the town of Berg on Lake Starnberg, who works in a Munich biscuit factory and has been a successful black-marketeer for a few weeks now, who has written poetry and literary criticism for the *Münchner Neueste Nachrichten*—is also standing spellbound, listening to Eisner. It is Oskar Maria Graf. He's there with his friend, the artist Georg Schrimpf, who painted the cover picture for Graf's first poetry collection, *The Revolutionaries*. It contained a short verse called "Adage":

> Sometimes we must be murderers;
> Humility has only defiled us all,
> And time passed us by, mantled in too much weariness.
> Hard-knocked, bowed by drudgery
> Fate's mercenary grits his teeth
> And blindly hurls himself into the teeming flood
> He will be purified
> And rise again a raw, sleepless penitent,
> Knowing his final mission...

For almost two years, the pair attended the pre-revolutionary Monday meetings at the Golden Anchor tavern in Ludwigsvorstadt, where Kurt Eisner was a regular speaker. That's where they know him from, albeit at a distance. "Good God, the whole of Munich is here," says Graf. "This is a real opportunity! I hope they don't just go home again today without taking some action." A bearded, uniformed giant hears and flashes him a supercilious smile. "Oh no, we ain't goin' home today... Goin' somewhere else today... Any minute now."

At that moment the people around them start shouting "Peace!" and "Long live the world revolution!" and "Long live Eisner!" Then silence descends for a minute and from further up the hill, from Bavaria, where the conciliatory Auer is speaking, the sound of cheering reaches them. Eisner's close friend Felix Fechenbach, a twenty-five-year-old writer with a doughy face and a sparse beard, calls out to the throng: "Comrades! Our leader Kurt Eisner has spoken! There's no sense in wasting any more words! If you're for the revolution, follow us! Follow me! March!"

The crowd surges forward as one, up the slope, heading for the Westend. On they go, past shops with their shutters pulled down, on towards the barracks. Graf and his friend Georg, whom everyone calls Schorsch, are marching almost at the head of the column, just five paces away from Eisner. Graf will later say of the man who has suddenly become their leader: "He was pale and his expression deadly serious; he didn't speak a word. It almost looked as if the sudden turn of events had taken him by surprise. Now and then he would stare straight ahead, half fearful and half distracted. He was walking arm in arm with the broad-shouldered, blind peasant leader Gandorfer, who strode along purposefully. His movements were much freer, he was heavy-footed and solid, and walked just as you'd imagine a Bavarian peasant might. The two of them were surrounded by a vanguard of loyal followers."

There are more and more of them. The police have fallen back, windows are opening, people looking out, silent, curious. The first armed men join the march, the mood is bright, as if they're going to a festival. Someone tells them the seamen have taken the Residence, there is an effervescent cheer, the excitement grows.

Where are they marching to? Their pale, determined leader seems to be following a schedule. They head resolutely further out of the city. Eventually the crowd plunges down a dark alley. Halt! comes the cry from the front. Where are they now? A school?

It's the Guldein School, which for the past few years has been used as a war barracks. The first shot is fired, people are on the edge of panic, some rush into the school, most push their way back out. Before long a window on the top floor of the school building is thrown open, and someone waves a red flag and shouts: "The men are for the revolution! They've all come over! Onward! March! March on!"

That is the moment. From then on, everything seems to happen of its own accord. More and more soldiers join them, they have torn the epaulettes from their shoulders, tied scraps of red cloth to their uniforms, a new community is forming. Children walk alongside the crowd, cheering. At one point they meet a soldier coming the other way, a paymaster, still wearing his insignia. They rip off his epaulettes, shove him from one person to the next. A giant of a man wants to lay hands on him. The soldier starts to weep and the brawny Oskar Maria Graf steps in: "Let him go! Come on, it's not his fault!" It takes some effort to placate the giant, who eventually mutters that Graf is right, but then also says: "Mind though, can't afford to be too kind!"

They march on from one barracks to the next. The same scene plays out again and again. A few men go in while Eisner and the others wait outside, and at some point a window opens and a red flag emerges. Cheering in the street; the crowd waits for their own people and the men they are bringing with them from the barracks, and then on they go.

After a while the group splits. They have heard the Maximilian II Barracks on Dachauer Straße is going to give them trouble. Shots are being fired there. That spurs on the group around Oskar Maria Graf, and they hurry on. When the sentry at the gate catches sight of the men, he drops his gun and runs away. The revolutionaries walk in. An officer has assembled a small troop in the exercise yard and is putting them through their paces, his back to the main gate. He doesn't even manage to turn around before someone hits him full-force over the head, ramming his helmet down far below his ears. At the same time, the soldiers abandon their weapons and run to the revolutionaries. "It's over! Revolution! March!" they cry.

Events are gathering pace, the people finding a sudden energy despite their exhaustion. The bloody war has lasted more than four years. They aren't just going to let it burn out and leave them in this twilight. Something bright and new has to—*has to*—come out of the darkness.

An Alpine herdsman whoops as if he is dancing a thigh-slapping *Schuhplatteln*, and a soldier on the fringes of the crowd gives an impromptu speech calling for the formation of soldiers' councils. The crowd presses on, to the military prison. Soldiers batter the locked gate with hatchets and rifle butts until it gives way, seemingly of its own accord. Later, Graf recalls: "I can still see in my mind's eye the cell doors opening and the prisoners coming out. One looked at us, wide-eyed and strange—he flinched and then suddenly broke into heart-breaking sobs. Then he fell wearily onto the breast of a short man and clung to him. Over and over, he howled: 'Thank you! Thank you! God bless you, God bless you!'"

Cell after cell is opened. The inmates stream out and join the crowd, which finally turns back towards the city centre. On Isartorplatz, Graf bursts into a hair salon where his friend Nanndl is working. He calls out to her: "Revolution! Revolution! Victory is ours!" She beams and drops the curling iron, but Graf is already gone.

The procession splits up; people keep stopping at the roadside to give speeches, and the streets of Munich's old town are too narrow to hold them all. Where now? Where will the republic be proclaimed?

Graf and Schorsch have come adrift from the main crowd. They cross over the River Isar to the Franziskaner beer hall. People are saying Eisner will speak there later. They order sausages and beer, ready for Eisner's revolutionary speech. But conviviality still reigns in the Franziskaner. Someone shouts: "Hey Wally, a pork knuckle over here!" No one is talking about politics, councils, the king, the war. Just beer and sausages and tobacco. Is no one here going to get fired up? What a comfortable, convivial people the Bavarians are!

When the two revolutionaries leave the Franziskaner, sated and merry, and turn back towards the old town, the streets are a bustle of activity. Everyone has heard some rumour or other. Evening promenaders are promenading up and down outside the Residence. Is the king still there? Will they see him one last time? Will they be present when the last of the Wittelsbach line leaves his city palace, where his family has reigned uninterrupted for 900 years? Oskar Maria Graf savours the new air and the possibilities hanging over the city, and above all the approaching end of this long, long war.

In the meantime, the main contingent has moved on to the Mathäserbräu beer hall, between the central railway station and Stachus Square. Nine in the evening, and there are sausages and beer and pork knuckles here too, but no cosy conviviality, only an industrious hum, eager concentration, astonishment and resolve. A workers' council is voted in, a soldiers' and a peasants' council too, organs of self-government, modelled on the Russian Soviets.

The blind peasant leader Ludwig Gandorfer is always at Kurt Eisner's side. Eisner is adamant that the peasants should be involved in the new government. The food supply situation in Munich is already difficult. If the peasants are not on their side and the people go hungry, then the revolution will be over in just a few days.

Outside, in front of the Mathäserbräu, lorries loaded with guns and ammunition are arriving and leaving. When soldiers and workers turn up, they are given weapons and sent off in small groups by the revolutionary council to occupy the city's public buildings.

Ministries, the central station, the army headquarters—one site after another falls into the revolutionaries' hands. Men wearing red armbands stride around the city. They are going to turn all of Munich red, red and new and peaceful and free.

In the Wittelsbach palace, the family seat of Ludwig III, there is chaos, dissolution, horror, bafflement. Where is the palace guard? Disbanded. Where are the royal troops to put an end to the terror outside? Prime Minister von Dandl and Minister of the Interior von Brettreich report to the king. No, this could not have been anticipated. Yes, Auer, the leader of the Social Democrats, assured them there would be no revolution. No, there is nothing to be done now and it would be best for the king and his family to leave the city immediately.

Then everything happens very quickly. The queen is ill with a fever; her physician has just been to see her. That doesn't make matters any easier. Where should they flee to? They settle on Castle Wildenwart near the Chiemsee. But how to get there? The first chauffeur has gone over to the revolutionaries. The second is with his sick wife. He is called in. The ailing queen learns of their imminent flight at her dressing table. The king has an old valet help him into his grey hunting coat, lined with possum fur. He tucks a box of cigars under his arm and is ready. The princesses Helmtrud, Hildegard, Gundelinde and Wiltrud, the queen, two gentleman courtiers, a baroness and the lady-in-waiting come to join him. The little royal group slips out of the city under cover of darkness.

By then, Kurt Eisner and his faithful followers have left the Mathäserbräu and are on their way to the Landtag, the state parliament in Prannerstraße. The night porter stops them on their way into the labyrinthine building, a large bunch of keys in his hand. No, he's not letting anyone in now, it's the middle of the night, and he's not about to surrender the keys either. A worker steps up and claps him on the shoulder: "Now then my friend, let's not cause a scene. Don't you know what hour is at hand?" The confused porter looks at his watch to check; the worker grows impatient, says no, he wasn't asking for the time, calls the porter an old fool and snatches the keys from him.

The small revolutionary troop leaves the bewildered keymaster behind and heads towards the debating chamber. The worker tries a few keys, finally finds the right one and they go in, Eisner, purposeful and self-assured, striding straight up to the prime minister's rostrum. At his side are Felix Fechenbach and the dramatist and journalist Wilhelm Herzog, the husband of the celebrated film diva Erna Morena, who has just been appointed by Eisner as the new government's Press Secretary and Chief Censor.

Eisner sits down in the prime minister's seat; Fechenbach and Herzog take the secretaries' chairs to either side. Workers stream into the chamber, a few women carrying red parasols. "It was a picturesque scene," Herzog later recalls. The noise, the excitement, the whispering, the shouts, the expectation, the disbelief, the joy, the Bavarian parliament in the middle of the night.

Kurt Eisner looks down at all the people. He brushes his long hair back from his forehead. He is standing up now, and soon he will speak, proclaim himself provisional Prime Minister and Bavaria a free state.

But for a moment he just watches. Is he casting his mind back? To his early days as a writer, his first book about Friedrich Nietzsche in 1892, when very little had been written about the man and his philosophy? To his critique of what he had called Nietzsche's "religion of hardness", which was "anti-socialist in its misanthropy"? When Eisner, even then, had considered socialism "a clear and achievable goal".

He had worked as a journalist for the Herold telegraph service, then as a sub-editor for the *Frankfurter Zeitung*, but already his ambition was driving him towards higher things. He wanted to review books, write leading articles, he asked for an interview with Leopold Sonnemann, the founder of that renowned paper. To no avail.

Eisner went to the regional *Hessische Landeszeitung* in Marburg and wrote articles that were admired throughout Hessen, in which he confidently mocked Wilhelmine politics, landed gentry and the feudal system. At the start of 1897, when one of his articles was a little over-confident, he was sent to

Plötzensee prison for nine months for *lèse-majesté*. He had written: "Give us a population of free, strict and demanding judges, and we might become king ourselves."

Is he recalling these lines now, as he suddenly finds himself on the throne? Or is he thinking of what came after his imprisonment? He had been hired at once by *Vorwärts*, the influential newspaper of the Social Democratic Party (SPD). He was responsible for the Sunday supplement, which he called "Sunday chatter", a mix of private and political topics, family and party.

But he had numerous enemies on the paper, especially among the elite and the party functionaries. Rosa Luxemburg, Victor Adler, Karl Kautsky, Franz Mehring: they called him a fanatic, a madman, a fantasist, a literary aesthete. Once, when he had heaped overly fulsome praise on a speech by August Bebel, Bebel wrote to him saying that Eisner's admiration was exaggerated, and that his enthusiasm embarrassed him. He was sacked from *Vorwärts* in 1905.

After that, he wrote for the *Fränkische Tagespost* and the *Münchener Post*, and moved to Munich with his family. In recent years he has appeared in public, speaking out against the war, with increasing frequency. His own party, the SPD, was pro-war. It approved war bonds in parliament, and any opposition to them from within the party's ranks was viewed as treason against the Fatherland.

Then, in April 1917, there was a split. A new national Independent Social Democratic Party (USPD) was founded in Gotha. The new party's main aim was to end the war and win back international trust. Kurt Eisner attended the first party conference, kept taking the floor, and became one of the leading personalities in this new anti-war party.

And the war was really over! It was finally over! Had everything now suddenly become reality? Had art become reality?

His dreams of art, which he had written about in all his theatre criticism? His speech in Berlin that year, when he talked
about Beethoven's Ninth Symphony and recalled that, "On
18th March 1905, to commemorate the March Revolution
and Friedrich Schiller, Beethoven's Ninth Symphony was
performed to the proletariat in a Berlin brewery hall, in the
middle of the workers' quarter. For the first time in history.
Almost 3,000 people were packed into the hot, overcrowded
hall—silent, reverential, doing their best to understand." The
proletariat, he went on, was now too strong and too mature
to keep allowing itself to be patronized in matters of high art.
"Everywhere, it is reaching for great heights, for the stars."
And: "A sense of release welled up from the depths. Joy!"

He had put all his dreams and convictions into this
Beethoven speech. All that he wanted to fight for. "Art is no
longer an escape from life; it is life itself," he proclaimed. And
finally, he laid out his vision: "If mankind, having achieved
freedom and maturity through the struggle of proletarian
socialism, is one day reared on the global hymn of the Ninth,
if it should become the catechism of their souls, then and
only then will Beethoven's art have returned to the home
from which it once fled: to life."

His new book, which he had completed and prepared for
printing while he was in prison following the strike in the
munitions factories, is to bear the title *Dreams of the Prophet*.
Yes, Kurt Eisner is a dreamer and a prophet. And he has spent
a long time fighting and writing for this moment in the
Bavarian Landtag.

He has to pull himself together. He has to give his speech.
At his side, Fechenbach is a little nervous. Eisner is not a
good public speaker. He thinks too much, his thoughts lack

structure and all too often he flounders, surprised by his own pathos.

But when Kurt Eisner starts to speak he is assured, firm and clear, "with a fiery temper, and the effect of his words could be read on every face". He talks for twenty minutes, completely off the cuff. Even the two men in the secretaries' seats to either side of him are so captivated that they fail to take notes. No one takes notes. Kurt Eisner's revolutionary speech, in which he declares Bavaria a free state and himself the head of its government, is undocumented.

Later, Herzog recalls a few lines. He says that Eisner began: "The Bavarian Revolution has triumphed. It has swept away the dead wood of the Wittelsbach kings." And then he hands power to himself: "The man who is speaking to you at this moment presupposes your agreement to his assuming the role of provisional Prime Minister." Cheering breaks out on the benches below. Eisner takes that as confirmation that he is now Prime Minister; he goes on, calling on everyone to stand united and keep the peace.

When he has finished, he lowers himself back into the prime-ministerial seat. Then he beckons Herzog to him and whispers in his ear: "We've forgotten the most important thing. The proclamation. Draft the wording, please. Quickly. Then we'll go into a side room and look through it together."

While Wilhelm Herzog is drafting the proclamation and Eisner is gazing pensively down at his people, far away on the Trudering road the royal family is slowly making its way towards Rosenheim. The night is foggy, the driver can hardly see the way ahead, and the car suddenly comes off the road and gets stuck in a potato field. All efforts to heave it out are in vain. The king, his cigars, his wife and his daughters are not going anywhere. The chauffeur sets off on foot to fetch help. The royal family is left in a field, in total darkness. Eventually the chauffeur comes back with some soldiers who are billeted in a nearby farmhouse, and a couple of horses. He also has a paraffin lamp. The sick farmer's wife, whom he met in the yard, didn't want to give it to him, but he finally managed to buy it from her for twenty marks. The horses pull the car out of the field—it immediately threatens to sink back into the mud on the other side of the road, but after a while they manage to right it. They drive on, cautiously and quietly, through the night.

At four o'clock the next morning, the family reaches Castle Wildenwart. They left home as royalty and have arrived as ordinary citizens.

"The Wittelsbach dynasty is hereby deposed." These are the final words of the proclamation that Wilhelm Herzog has written out in a side room off the debating chamber. He rushed it to Kurt Eisner just before midnight; the latter read it over and, to Herzog's surprise, largely approved it. There were just two or three sentences he wanted to change. And then: out with it to the telegraph offices and the newsrooms. Eisner has added a handwritten note: "To be printed on the 1st page (front page)."

"Fellow countrymen!" it says in giant letters at the top of the page. "In order to rebuild after long years of destruction, the people have overturned the power of the civil and military authorities and taken government into their own hands. The Bavarian government is hereby proclaimed."

Looking at the little group who were left in the debating chamber, did Eisner have a moment of doubt as to whether these people were really "the people"? Perhaps not. His happiness was too great, the chance to realize his dreams had come to him too suddenly and too easily. And there was no time for reflection now, in any case: he had far too much to do.

For example, the editor-in-chief of the *Münchner Neueste Nachrichten*, the large Munich daily paper, now bursts into the parliament building. He is denied entry to the chamber, and a worker brings Eisner the irate man's visiting card. "You talk to him," Eisner tells Wilhelm Herzog. "And by the by, we don't have a press censor yet. As of now, that will be your responsibility." And he writes down the new post he has just given Herzog on a slip of paper. An impromptu identity card for the Chief Censor of the new People's Republic.

Very well then: Herzog agrees, and strides out to see the furious editor, who roars that the whole of his publishing house and print works are occupied, it's a catastrophe, if this situation continues the paper won't come out tomorrow, or at least not punctually, which would be the first time that has happened since it was founded in 1848.

"Yes, well," says Herzog, "we haven't had a revolution in Bavaria since then, either." In any case, he says, it really wouldn't be such a catastrophe if just this once people got their morning paper at nine or ten o'clock rather than six. "At least then, they will notice something has changed."

The Chief Censor is handed some copies of the proclamation. He gives one to editor-in-chief Müller, tells him to print it, and says his paper can come out as normal.

But how? The whole place is still occupied by those ruffians with the red armbands. When Müller gets back to the editorial offices and the printing shop, he does at least see that everything is once again running in an orderly fashion. The revolutionaries are allowing his staff to get on with their nocturnal work.

But where is he going to put the proclamation? The editor in charge of the machines has an idea. There is currently a full-page advert on the second page. He stops the machines, swaps the current page one to page two, and the news of the day goes on the front page, as instructed by the new government: "To the people of Munich!" it begins. There follows a brief account of the night's events from the revolutionaries' point of view, and then: "From this moment on, Bavaria is a free state. A people's government, borne up by the faith of the masses, shall be appointed without delay." It goes on: "A new age is upon us! Bavaria wants to prepare Germany for the League of Nations. The democratic and social Republic of Bavaria has the moral strength to bring about a peace for Germany that will protect it from the worst."

This text is also designed to have a placatory, reassuring effect on the populace, assuring it that the "strictest order" will be maintained through the Workers', Soldiers' and Peasants' Councils. "The safety of people and property is guaranteed." It is an appeal to everyone, to every man and woman in Munich: "Workers and citizens of Munich! Trust in the great and mighty future we are shaping in these momentous days! You can help to make the unavoidable transformation quick and easy [...] Every human life is sacred. Keep the peace and play your part in building this new world!" Signed by Kurt Eisner, in the early morning of 8th November 1918, in the Bavarian Landtag.

Shortly before this, at around midnight, the leader of the Social Democrats Erhard Auer and the union secretary Schiefer come to see Brettreich, the Minister of the Interior. The minister has summoned Auer. Hadn't Auer given him his word that he need fear no revolutionary uprising? That order would be maintained? A demonstration, a little music, and then every-one would disperse peacefully. Had Auer lied to him? Did he not have his people under control?

In fact, Brettreich already knows what has happened. Auer really did lead his calm, well-disciplined little group back into the city that afternoon and send his people home. No one was angrier than Auer at the fact that the Independents and the Communists had gone to the barracks with Eisner and then, like the denouement of some beer-hall comedy, had got themselves elected to government in the Mathäserbräu by a few of their fighting comrades and drinking companions, with shouting and tankards held aloft.

And now, three men look helplessly at each other. Auer says that the government should have brought order over the course of the day. Brettreich says he no longer has any power over his people. Auer says the government needs to put down the uprising before morning. After that, the workforce will restore order by itself. The men part company. There is nothing for them to do. What will happen, will happen. Without them.

The revolutionaries still have much to do on this night.

The police headquarters is not yet in the hands of the upris-ing. Eisner sends Fechenbach off to see to that. Fechenbach sees to it. He hurries over to the headquarters, which is full of policemen standing around in little groups, discussing the events of the previous day and night. His red armband opens all doors to him. He goes from room to room, until he finally reaches the office of Chief of Police Rudolf von Beckh, who has gathered his section heads there for a meeting. Fechenbach explains that the councils have just taken provisional control of the government and would like to instruct him, the Chief of Police, to continue as head of the security services until they are reorganized. A police supervisory board will be appointed in the course of the night. And right now, he must sign a declaration for Fechenbach stating that he will follow all orders issued by the councils. The Chief of Police requests some time to think. There is complete silence in the room as the section heads look at each other awkwardly, then he makes up his mind, writes a declaration of loyalty on a sheet of paper and adds: "If I should be unable to fulfil this commitment, I must reserve the right to step down. Munich, 8th November 1918, 1 a.m. Chief of Police von Beckh."

That night Josef Staimer, a former warehouseman, union secretary and current head of the Soldiers' Council, is assigned to von Beck to oversee his work; the next morning, this man is made Chief of Police himself.

On this curious night, things seem to happen of their own accord. Power over the state simply falls to Kurt Eisner and his people.

And who is this now, arriving at the Landtag at two in the morning and getting through to see the Prime Minister? A young artillery officer, out of breath, red-faced, stands before Eisner and says: "I've come from Schleißheim, where there are eight hundred men, twenty guns and a few howitzers. All at your service!" To which Eisner replies: "Excellent! Bring them all here and station the artillery outside the building."

So this forgotten problem also appears to have solved itself, for the time being. The city's troops were, after all, disbanded in the afternoon. And even if many of the soldiers are on the side of the revolutionaries, or at least not on the side of the old king, there still isn't a single functioning unit under the new government's command. The soldiers are all just roaming around or sitting in beer halls, or they've gone home. Now the Schleißheim troops will provide a minimal level of protection for the first days of the regime.

And now it is three o'clock in the morning. Kurt Eisner, the new ruler of Bavaria, the wild-haired theatre critic who recognized his moment so quickly and seized it with such determination, is tired. His friend Fechenbach has found a sofa in one of the meeting rooms for parliamentary groups. He and Wilhelm Herzog counsel the Prime Minister to sleep for a little while.

"Where?" asks Eisner. "On the benches, where the honourable members of parliament liked to sleep?"

"No," says Fechenbach. "We've found a room with a day bed for you. You can lie down for an hour there."

He takes Eisner to the meeting room. As the people's king flops exhausted onto the sofa, he says: "Is this not miraculous? We have staged a revolution without spilling a drop of blood! There has never been such a thing in history."

Outside on the streets of Munich, silence has long since fallen. An occasional shot is fired in the night. The stars are out. A drunk man in a dark overcoat staggers alone through the streets of Schwabing. "Movement! Bang! Bang! Bang!" he crows into the night. "Mooove-ment!" Does anyone hear him?

It is Oskar Maria Graf, filling the night with noise. In the evening he lost sight of the action, getting to the Mathäserbräu too late and then hurrying over to the royal Residence just as the king was leaving through another exit.

There, Graf met his best black-market customer, Anthony van Hoboken, a fabulously wealthy Dutchman. In the last few weeks he has bought ox tongues, wine, butter and other rare delicacies from Graf, who gets them from a shady wholesaler. Hoboken—Graf just calls him the sheep-faced Dutchman—comes from a Rotterdam banking family. He has a great love of literature, an even greater love of music, and most of all he loves private parties with female artists, painters, witty writers who live large and drink heavily. After concluding their business, he has often asked Graf to stay and have a drink. And Graf has had a drink. Every time.

Now they spot each other from a distance, wave, and Graf calls out to him: "The glory days are over now!" He actually means the Dutchman and his money and grandeur and high living. But the Dutchman himself seems to be in fine spirits, splendidly entertained by the city's revolutionary mood. The lover at his side cries out in a little girl's voice: "Yes, isn't it fabulous!"

She is a sparkling person who calls herself Marietta of Monaco. Her real name is Maria Kirndörfer and she is a petite, fine-boned twenty-five-year-old who grew up with foster parents in Munich, attended a convent school, spent some time on the streets and was discovered by chance as an elocutionist in 1913 in the Schwabing cabaret bar Simplicissimus. During the war she went to Zurich and became one of the founding members of Cabaret Voltaire. She used to introduce herself with a little piece she called "Who am I?"

> I am a bright bouncing ball.
> Rich boys roll me across silken rugs.
> Children coo over me.
> I slip through the elegant fingers of notable people.
> But sometimes rough lads come and play football.
> Then I sail from their shoes into the crystal bowl of
> The most noble queen.

She has been back in Munich for some time, singing and declaiming in the Schwabing bars favoured by artists, which are now all revolutionary bars, and slipping through the elegant fingers of this notable Dutchman. People call her the "muse of Schwabylon". Everyone who sees her is entranced.

Marietta and the Dutchman, then, are delighted by the night's events, and Graf, who was convinced that the primary targets of this revolution would be the bigwigs, parasites and millionaires, is momentarily surprised. How terribly his poverty has made him suffer! He became father to a baby girl in June and is unhappily married to Karoline Bretting—very unhappily married, from the first day on. But until he came up with his black-market scheme, his greatest suffering was caused by always being short of money. "Over time, money really became something like a demon for me, and it ruled my life. Everything the poets and philosophers went on about was all nonsense: morality, ethics and strength of character, idealism and God knows what other good qualities. These qualities were ultimately all subordinate—money made them or snuffed them out. Mankind had invented something to which, over time, he inevitably surrendered himself, body and soul," he wrote later.

Might the revolution now take this devilish invention and simply—abolish it? Wasn't that inevitable, in fact? So why were this sheep-faced man and his muse of Schwabylon so cock-a-hoop?

But Graf didn't care now. The world had begun to teeter, a new world was emerging at long last, and he just wanted to celebrate. He went home with the Dutchman and Marietta, they drank and drank late into the night, and Graf finally staggered home in the early hours of the morning. The streets of Schwabing were empty and silent; now and then a shot echoed through the night. The revolution was asleep.

When Graf gets home, he writes a letter to his wife: "I don't like you any more! I never liked you! It was all just lies and pity! Let me be! Let us go our separate ways!" Everything has broken open, in the city and within him, too; outside everything has changed, and now he has to change as well. He is in love with someone else, he calls her "the girl", or sometimes "the black girl": Mirjam Sachs, with her black eyes and her soft face. She is studying in Munich but comes from Berlin, and is a friend of the poet Rainer Maria Rilke. She, the black girl, is who Graf wants to live with. No more lies, no more pity, no more compromises. The letter is finished. He leaps up from the table. What he has written is sheer madness. He tears it up, gets into bed and falls asleep, the night's last revolutionary. Drunk. Married. Ready for a new land. A new life.

A slender, delicate man with large eyes and large lips spent the evening in quite a different way. With a young woman who calls herself Elya, Elya like the king's daughter from the old Augsburg St George mystery play that she had acted in a few weeks earlier. He had seen her in it. "Rilke's here," her partner had whispered to her while they were still on stage. And the next day: "Rilke's here again." And on the day of the final performance: "Rilke wants to come up to the stage after the show. He wants to meet you."

But then he had not come after all, and she had written him a letter, the man whose poems she knew by heart—they had been a life to her. She knew him already from his words, was close to him without ever having met him: "Rainer Maria," she wrote, "once I loved your soul almost as one loves God. That was when I first read the *Book of Hours*." And she ended: "Can just one soul not live larger, this depressing workaday life—larger and more inwardly."

Rilke replied at once, inviting her to Schwabing, to his fourth-floor apartment in Ainmillerstraße where he read to her and sat in silence with her. In her letters she addressed him, quoting his poems, as: "God, Thou art great" and "Thou immortal". He said: "When I think of you I see us kneeling side by side as in a dream, and that may well be our relationship to one another. When will you come and see me again?"

Rilke liked to kneel with his admirers, his sweethearts, his lovers. To kneel in admiration before a work of art, an altar, until their eyes brimmed with tears.

The poet Rainer Maria Rilke had almost fallen silent during the war. He wrote hardly any poems after being called up for military service and sent to Vienna at the start of 1916. Although influential friends got him released after just six months, the military exercises had shaken this slender, almost transparent man to the core.

After that, he went to stay with some rich friends on an island, the Herreninsel in the Chiemsee, then spent a few months in Berlin, financially dependent on aristocratic ladies and the wives of captains of industry. In Berlin, he also met these ladies' husbands: Detlev, Count von Moltke, the Kaiser's aide-de-camp; Richard von Kühlmann, Secretary of State for Foreign Affairs who in early 1918 would go on to negotiate the peace of Brest-Litovsk with revolutionary Russia; Walther Rathenau, head of the electrical engineering company AEG and later Foreign Minister in the Weimar Republic. The Establishment figures of the German Empire met with the author of the *Book of Hours* and *The Notebooks of Malte Laurids Brigge* because their wives loved him, because he was a true independent, a listener, a taciturn, moral man whom these powerful gentlemen trusted.

In summer 1917, the silent poet had met a young Russian woman in the royal palace of Herrenchiemsee. Her husband was a political prisoner in Berlin; she was Sophie Liebknecht, the wife of the German Communist Party's leader. The two became friends. Rilke, who had a deep love of Russia, liked Sophie a great deal for her heritage alone. He complained to her of how the war was making him suffer, and she told him his suffering would be easier to bear "if you did not spurn the times in which we live, if you paid more attention to them, read newspapers and took more interest, and thus developed a more real relationship with them". She was sure he could go on writing then—"and after all, that is the most important thing to you".

Read the papers. Think about politics. Take heed of reality. Somehow be *in our time*! Not like the panther in Paris's Jardin des Plantes, about which he had written at the start of the century:

> To him, there seem to be a thousand bars
> And out beyond those thousand bars, no world.

But Rilke *was* in the world. And he was much too permeable for these daily catastrophes. There was too much happening in the world, brutality, noise everywhere, war.

The war that he, like all of Europe, had welcomed with such naivety, drunk with joy:

> A god at last! Since the God of Peace often
> Escaped our grasp, the Battle God has grasped us,
> Hurling flames; and over a heart full of home
> He dwells thunderous in his screaming, crimson heaven.

Yes, that poem was written by a man who looked as if a strong gust of wind would suffice to blow him out of his gaiters. He was carried away by the Battle God. But not for long. "Three months after that I saw the spectre—and now, for how long now, it has been nothing but the evil effluvium from the human swamp," he wrote just one year later. And fell silent.

No, he was not an active opponent of war. He suffered quietly. He wrote to the wife of his publisher, Anton Kippenberg, after the October Revolution in 1917, saying that he was sustained only by "the thought of glorious Russia". He had loved Russia since his early travels to that longed-for eastern land, loved Russian poetry, had a lot of Russian friends, especially female friends, and the revolution filled him with hope that the war would end, that a new age would begin.

He knew Kurt Eisner and held him in high regard. Rilke had written to him at the start of 1918, seeking advice on behalf of a female friend who wanted to set up a relief organization for the poor. The letter didn't reach Eisner at the time: he was in jail following the strike by munitions workers that he had helped to bring about.

Rilke, a man removed from the times he lived in, the darling of the wealthy and the old aristocracy, and dependent on them, too, was ready for the new age—more than ready. On 24th October 1918 he wrote to his ex-wife, Clara Westhoff-Rilke, with a motto to be written on the hand-carved beams of her house in Fischerhude, near Bremen:

When all was falling, self-belief began.
The future says I may. I know I can.

In the final days of the war, Rilke plunges into life, into the assembly halls of Munich. "I have been going out every evening until late for some days now, and the same today and tomorrow as well," he writes on 3rd November to his princess Elya. He sends his elegies, the poems he began before the war and will complete years later, when they will be published under the title *Duino Elegies*, to his publisher in Leipzig for safe keeping, away from what is happening in Munich. Because anything might happen now. And he wants to be there. He will be there.

The following day, on 4th November, the famous Heidelberg professor Max Weber comes to the city. He is an opponent of the war and of the revolution, a left-leaning liberal who advocates a parliamentary system like the one in England.

And three days after that, Rilke's excitement can be read in every line he writes to Clara in Fischerhude:

> On Monday evening I was with thousands of others in the halls of the Hotel Wagner; the speaker was Professor Max Weber from Heidelberg, national economist, who is regarded as one of the best minds and a good orator. Afterwards, in the discussion, the overwrought anarchist Mühsam spoke, and then students, men who had been four years at the front, all so simple and open and plain-speaking [...] The haze of beer and smoke and people was not stifling, one was hardly aware of it, so important was the discussion, and above all it was immediately clear that people could finally say the things that needed to be said. The simplest and truest of these things, when they were put at least to some degree in plain language, were greeted by the enormous crowd with hearty, loud applause. Suddenly a pale-faced worker got up, spoke quite simply: "Did you, or you—did any of you", he said, "make the armistice offer? And yet we are the ones who ought to be doing it, not those gentlemen up there; if we take over a radio station and speak, ordinary folk to other ordinary folk, we will have peace in no time."

Oskar Maria Graf had been in the same hall on that 4th November 1918. The professor from Heidelberg had sent him into a white-hot rage. "A tall man, he stood there, large, gruff, solid, wearing a frock coat and looking like a Baden democrat," said Graf. The professor spoke against Bavaria's breakaway from Prussia, against militarism, but above all against revolution: "It is a nonsense, it would be a crime, it is impossible for bourgeois society to be transformed into a future state based on socialist principles by means of a revolution!" The people on the benches called "Oho!" but Weber would not let himself be cowed: "We would have the enemy in the country, and later a reaction of the worst kind!" he prophesied.

But this evening, that was something no one wanted to hear. The wild, bearded anarchist Erich Mühsam shouted that Weber should ask the troops on the front lines how they felt about peace, and he urged the women to demonstrate for peace again, to keep demonstrating. Finally Graf himself leapt up, trembling, and shouted into the hall, into the crowd, at the professor: "The revolution is coming! It's coming! I call on the soldiers to disobey orders and leave their barracks!" He sat back down to a chorus of cheers and boos.

Did Oskar Maria Graf see Rilke that evening? They knew each other, they liked each other very much: the rough, revolutionary people's poet and the gentle poet of the stars. Was this the evening that Graf would remember much later with such fondness? "In those eventful weeks of the Eisner revolution in Munich, he (Rilke) often went to loud, chaotic public meetings. No one knew him, and he preferred it that way. He never pushed forward to the speaker's lectern; he remained inconspicuous in the crush of people and disappeared again just as inconspicuously. 'Rilke', acquaintances whispered to each other as they saw him pass; they glanced after him, nodded shyly and were momentarily surprised. No one expected to see him there."

They will see each other more often in the coming weeks, in the transformed state of Bavaria. But perhaps it was on this evening that they walked side by side for a little while on their way home and Graf spoke of his doubts, his unease at the fact that the rural folk, the peasants, would not be involved in this great, important uprising. The peasants scorned all the clever, self-important speech-makers in the city because they were so clueless about real life, about work, earning money, milking cows, slaughtering cows and suchlike. And in fact these were the very people who *had* to be involved; the revolution was conceived and made for them and it would all be pointless if the peasants out in the countryside rejected the whole uprising, the whole of this beautiful new age. His hopes were pinned on the people, said Graf. And Rilke said quietly: "Yes, any benevolent person may hope... No one is able to see and feel something new yet, but we must be patient... 'The people' includes our kind, too—the people, without restriction or addition... So we have been told..."

Rilke did not stop attending the public meetings. An end to the war was his greatest hope, and he was prepared to be swept along in spirit by the new age, by the revolution, even if he also feared it. "For more than four years we stood in that fiery glow," he writes on 6th November to the actress Anni Mewes, "And all our lights have gone out to such a degree that when the war is extinguished, it will leave us in the most terrible darkness there has ever been, unless in their desperation the people light another mighty fire, the sparks of which are already kindling little flames here and there on the fringes of the crowd. And to think that the luminance of intellectual life will be as feeble in this new atmosphere as it was for four years in wartime air!"

He hopes things will turn out differently. This "luminance of intellectual life" is where he has placed his faith and he knows that, in this, Kurt Eisner is on his side. But will the people see things the same way? "Art", he goes on, "always promises the most distant future—the one after next, at the soonest—and for that reason a crowd which is passionately reaching for the next one will always be iconoclastically minded."

Fear is mixed with hope. Rilke cannot understand why the old rulers don't recognize the deadly danger that threatens both them and the old power structures, and why they don't come out to meet the people. They will be too late to avert their own downfall. He writes to his publisher Kippenberg's royalist wife, on the very day before the king is deposed, saying that he believes a revolution might still be prevented if the government can gain more popular appeal. But he has grave doubts about that: "It will be the downfall of the man who comes too late, if it should prove that the long-neglected will of the people can now only draw breath in a mighty explosion." Those who come too late are punished by life. Rilke saw everything very clearly.

And then, when the will of the people really does explode the following evening, the poet is at a concert with his pretend princess, Elya, a Lieder evening of "melodies from ages past and ancient times". "It was not really an evening to immerse oneself in 'ages past' or 'ancient times', when these (perhaps) came to an end yesterday," he will write a day later. A past age is ending, a great epoch, and a new one is rising. Rainer Maria Rilke listens to the sound of the past dying away.

The very next morning, he comments on the events of that "remarkable night", as he calls it: "Now all we can do is hope that this unaccustomed state of uprising puts people's minds into a reflective mood and does not tip them over into catastrophic intoxication. So far all seems calm, and one cannot help but concede that this is the time for trying to take great strides."

Thomas Mann, too, had been at a Lieder evening on 7th November. He was annoyed even as they set out that evening, because no trams were running. He'd been annoyed all day at the "ridiculous mob" marching through the city yelling "Republic!" and "Down with the dynasty!" And now he and his wife Katia had to get to the Türkenstraße concert hall on foot. Their seats were up in the gallery, where there was such a terrible draught that they went back down into the stalls. The composer Hans Pfitzner was conducting that night. He was an anti-democratic ultra-nationalist and a Wagnerian, who during the war had composed and premiered the opera *Palestrina*. Thomas Mann had attended four performances in a row. He was truly inspired by what he regarded as a perfect, and quintessentially Germanic, work of art. He had devoted pages and pages of his recently published book *Reflections of a Nonpolitical Man* to enthusing about this musician and this piece. Thomas Mann saw all the perfection of Wagner, of German Romanticism, in *Palestrina*: "What great artistry, in combination with the most nervous agility, penetrating harmonic audacity with a pious ancestral style!" In Pfitzner, he had discovered a true kindred spirit: German composer, anti-democratic invoker of general decline, romantic, artist, humorist. "Pessimism and humour—I have never perceived their correlation more strongly and never more sympathetically than in the face of the second Palestrina act. The optimist, the reformer, in a word, the politician is never a humorist; he is lofty-rhetorical."

In the *Reflections* Thomas Mann had rejected in the strongest terms words like politics, optimism, democracy, progress, civilization, claiming they were un-Germanic in the most profound sense. He had called the book a "general revision of my intellectual principles"; it was his war service, carried out from behind a desk. It was a defensive book: against France, against the threat of defeat, against democracy, against his brother, the early democrat Heinrich Mann, whom he openly vilified as a "literatus of civilization", and who he says exhibits every ridiculous, dangerous, anti-German emotion there is.

The book has only just been published. At the worst possible time. He had telegraphed his publisher Samuel Fischer at the last minute to try and stop it being distributed. The publisher replied at once, saying that unfortunately it was too late: distribution had already begun. "God damn it all," Mann writes in his diary—a sigh of resignation.

So at the very moment when everything is pointing towards defeat for Germany and a victory for democracy, Thomas Mann, whose greatest goal is to be Germany's most representative writer, brings out a fundamentally anti-democratic work. This really is a very bad move.

But his principal concern is his feud with his older brother. Heinrich still knows nothing about this attack on him. A week before the book was distributed, Thomas Mann had a nightmare: "I dreamt I was somewhere with Heinrich on the best of terms, and out of goodwill let him eat up a great number of cakes, small a la crème ones and two pieces of torte, giving up my own share. Puzzled how this friendship relates to the publication of the *Betrachtungen*. I kept thinking this surely won't do, it is a totally impossible situation. On awakening, the feeling of relief that it was a dream."

Thomas Mann is extremely on edge during these days, and has been for months, while he was still writing the *Reflections*. The children—there are currently five of them—feel this most acutely. Whenever their father is working or sleeping or reading, absolute silence has to be maintained in the large new house on Poschingerstraße, overlooking the Herzogpark on the south bank of the Isar. And in fact he works and sleeps and reads all day, when he's not out with the dog, walking on the nearby riverbank. Golo, who is nine years old at the end of the war, later recalls: "We had to stay quiet practically all the time: in the morning because Father was working, in the afternoon because he was reading or napping, and towards evening because that was when he would start doing serious work again. If we ever disturbed him, we would get a fearful scolding."

He is even more on edge when Hans Pfitzner comes to see him. If he stays to dinner, the children aren't even allowed to sit at the table, because Pfitzner, as Klaus remembers, has "very raw nerves". Even his host, Pfitzner's greatest admirer, is rather unsettled by the visitor: "I doubt that he felt at ease," Thomas Mann wrote to his neighbour and friend, the musical director of the Munich Opera Bruno Walter, who had conducted the premiere of *Palestrina*, "although he drank at least five glasses of Moselle wine, consumed a great number of home-made biscuits and so at least in this regard reacted positively to what he was offered. In general, I suspect he never really feels at ease anywhere."

Thomas Mann did not let this dent his admiration one bit. What was he supposed to do? He had been deeply affected by this opera, which he regarded as a fraternal project to his *Reflections*. And when one evening, out on the terrace, Pfitzner described the prevailing voice of his work as one of "sympathy with death", the author of *Buddenbrooks* and *Death in Venice* was completely convinced. Sympathy with death: that was his theme, his motif, his temptation. That was the seductive power of German Romanticism, which was to be the downfall of the pale, wavering hero of his mountain novel, a book he had begun before the war and then set aside to work on the *Reflections*. Sympathy with death: that was Schubert's "Lindenbaum" song, it was Gustav von Aschenbach surrendering himself to his love for a boy, it was German music, German irresponsibility. Yes, *The Magic Mountain* should be permeated by this mood. The diligent engineer Hans Castorp, who only means to visit the magical mountain world for three weeks, will be infected by it and it will make him ill. He will be infected by love, music, inertia, his own reluctance to take an interest in politics. Sympathy with death: it was the opposite of everything that now seemed to threaten Germany—democracy, active participation in politics by ordinary people, responsibility. The opposite of the world in which Thomas Mann felt at home. The lowlands. The counter-world to the magic mountain.

He had completed just a few chapters of the novel before the war. And really, it was only supposed to be a novella, a counterpart to *Death in Venice*, but Mann had already realized that it was in danger of outgrowing that form, that the material would flood the banks of a novella. Now finally, after four years, he was thinking about taking it up again, forging ahead, climbing back into the mountains of Davos.

Forging ahead: that suited his present state of mind. He had just finished his dog story, the tale of Bauschan, the short-haired German pointer. "A Man and his Dog—an Idyll" is what he had called the story, and indeed it was. A tale simply told, of small, everyday kinds of happiness. For once he wasn't inventing, striving, struggling to shape the material—just letting his pen carry him forward from where he started: "When the beautiful season does credit to its name, and the warbling of the birds has been able to awaken me early because I ended the previous day at the proper time, I like to go out without my hat even before breakfast for a half-hour's walk down the avenue of trees in front of my house, or even to the more distant park areas, in order to draw a few breaths of the early-morning air and to participate to some extent in the pleasures of the fresh forenoon before my work occupies me fully."

But that was over now, too. He had written the final sentence on 14th October. The walk was at an end: "And then I hasten to go in and take off my hobnailed boots, because the soup is already on the table." That same day, Thomas Mann had heard about a soldier who'd arrived at the central station after a short furlough, intending to travel back to the front, but had been turned away. There are no more trains to the front now. Stay at home, lad, they'd told him.

Time too for Thomas Mann to recognize the direction history was taking. In these days, the whole country was a whirl of frenzied confusion and collapse, and the censored, royalist, pro-war press hadn't prepared people for it. Germany had marched from one victory to the next for four years, and now it was supposed to concede a total defeat? Thomas Mann vacillated. What was to become of his book? Of his life? Of his country? "Provided it is acknowledged beforehand (and I assume that the world, too, will acknowledge it) that Germany is the real victor in this war—insofar as 'war' is the proper word—there remains no other choice, and it is the only sensible and dignified choice, but to view things from the comic side and declare the victory of the virtuous Allies a colossal humbug."

A writer takes his leave of reality. It is simply wrong; it doesn't fit the world view he has painstakingly created. So: there *was* no war, he declares from on high, behind his desk. Germany is victorious, the world is a comedy, and this supposed victory for democracy is a huge joke.

All he can do now is hold his head up. Save his own empire. Defend it against France. Against Heinrich. All that's left is to retreat into his own universe. And now, he writes, his task is to "recognize and accept the political direction in which the world is moving, to salute the democratic new world with good grace as a kind of world convenience that it will be quite possible to live with [...] and keep everything cultural, national, philosophical separate from politics and free, on a plane high above politics, something not in the least affected by democratic utilitarianism".

But how do you escape this downward pull? When your own country and everything you believe in, everything you have fought for in your writing, has been defeated? Retreat, retreat. Thomas Mann thinks of *The Magic Mountain* and decides to forge ahead with it soon. But if he is honest, Thomas Mann has only one real desire in these turbulent days: "I don't wish to be impoverished, to that much I can testify."

He is absent, of course, from the beer halls of the pre-revolution. But he has his contacts, he gets reports. He hears about the mass meeting on 4th November at which Max Weber spoke and Erich Mühsam and Oskar Maria Graf shouted, "The revolution is coming!" Franz Ferdinand Baumgarten, a Hungarian essayist who wears a monocle, reports back to him the following day that "intellectual Munich" had been there, and that he and the young writer Hanns Johst had agreed "that this dreadful confusion of people talking over each other had given an impression of sadness, hopelessness and nationalistic, human bleakness". Mann adds in his diary with some satisfaction: "That certainly tallies with my own experiences."

This Hanns Johst is, however, not so very critical of the revolutionary movement. In these days, he sees in the people "a great deal of pure conviction" and the will to "force a new ideal into being". Fifteen years later Hanns Johst, by then president of the Prussian Academy of Arts' literature division, will warmly welcome the burning of books written by former colleagues. Two years after that he will be head of the Reich Writers' Union and preside over the official canon of German literature, newly reorganized along national, racial and political lines.

But all this still lies at the end of a long road. Thomas Mann summons people out to his house on the Isar, to bring him news from the city. The more depressing they make the situation seem, the more justified he feels in escaping to his idyll. That so-called reality out there has no bearing on him. Perhaps Monocle Baumgarten also tells him about Oskar Maria Graf's bluster at the meeting. And perhaps Thomas Mann then recalls that this Graf wrote to him just a few weeks earlier to tell him about a new project, a "magazine for new humanity and ethical literature" that he intended to start. He hoped so ardently for a kind word, said Graf, some support, some sign of goodwill from the acclaimed creator of *Buddenbrooks*. And Thomas Mann wrote him a very kindly postcard, welcoming the new venture and wishing him the best of luck. The young magazine founder was speechless with happiness. "I was on top of the world," he wrote.

And now, three days after that 4th November, Thomas Mann has been to Pfitzner's concert with his wife Katia, "not overwhelming, though it had its beautiful moments," he notes later. The two had actually agreed to have supper with Pfitzner later that evening in the Vier Jahreszeiten hotel. They didn't go in the end, but returned home accompanied by another composer, Walter Braunfels, who wrote the opera *Princess Brambilla*. Braunfels was not a nervous nationalist like his colleague Pfitzner, just a little highly strung when it came to religion. His Jewish father had converted to Protestantism, and Braunfels himself had just recently converted from Protestantism to Catholicism on his return from the war—a subject he was always talking about.

But not this evening. This evening there were a thousand rumours to be discussed on their walk home. Had the king really fled the city? Had the mob really thrown gas grenades into the Türkenstraße barracks? Hounded the soldiers out and ripped the imperial cockades from their uniforms? The soldiers they had encountered certainly weren't wearing their cockades any more. And what had happened after that? The police were nowhere to be seen. The mood was silent, tense; the sound of gunshots echoed through the night. Bruno Walter and his wife had rushed home in a state of high anxiety even before the Manns and Braunfels set off. The conductor feared for his house, his money, his life. Where were the police? Why was all this just being allowed to happen?

The Manns and their companion are taking a rather more relaxed view of things. In the past few days, Thomas Mann has swaddled himself in something like a magic cloak. His idyll, far away from all this. None of it—the mob, democracy, the war, the German defeat—has any bearing on him. From his lofty observation post he looks down at the German people, at so-called reality far below. "An ersatz Carnival" is what he calls the people's exertions, with a bitter laugh. Let them get on with it. What does it matter to him. The night is clear and cold. Thomas Mann stops for a moment, asks his companion to stand with him and cast a brief glance up at the skies. "Look at this beauty, this luminous eternal heaven," he says. "Eternity puts one in a contemplative mood," he adds solemnly, and then repeats the basic tenet he has adopted in recent days: "Fundamentally, what is human is alien to politics."

They walk home along the Isar. The lamps are lit in the villa at the end of Poschingerstraße. They have supper, drink a glass of punch, and together they decide not to take the whole thing too seriously.

Until the next morning. Thomas Mann has caught a cold; the long walk through the cold night has not done him any good. Now the sun breaks through the fog, and the telephone rings. It's Katia's mother, the self-assured, wealthy Hedwig Pringsheim, who has never quite taken her son-in-law seriously. She informs her daughter of the previous night's events, the king's flight, the proclamation of the Free State.

Then the *Münchner Neueste Nachrichten* arrives, two hours late, with its new front page. And Thomas Mann is a little surprised after all. He turns pale. He may well have underestimated the situation. He reads the proclamation on page one, signed by "colleague Eisner", as he notes in his diary. He reads with relief that colleague Eisner is guaranteeing "Strictest order, security of persons and private property". He hears gunfire in the distance. He sees his daughter, his beloved Elisabeth, lying outside on the lawn, and thinks that at the moment they are realized, all revolutions become essentially conservative, and therefore German. He thinks and thinks about how the new situation might be made to fit his old world view, his old dream.

In fact, this is not such a difficult task. "The German Revolution is after all German, though nonetheless a revolution," he writes. It is what it is. Thomas Mann is an instant conservative. As soon as the country has changed, he is immediately in favour of preserving the new status quo. Or tries to be, at least.

Is Eisner not a good man? Patriarchal, kindly, a little eccentric but well meaning enough, and actually a "colleague" in the best sense of the word, without any hint of irony. And is this not a good thing for the country? Will the mere existence of this moral government with its international outlook not ensure that the world makes a peace that is good for Germany?

Mann rehearses his new role in the new state through the daily declarations he makes in his diary: "I can say that my attitude towards future developments, if they really take the form I envision, is rather friendly, hopeful, receptive, consenting."

And he mocks his friend Bruno Walter, who is constantly afraid for his life and his money. Now, on the first afternoon of the republic, Walter tells the Manns with utter horror that a band of looters is approaching. Thomas Mann doesn't quite take it seriously, but still decides to remain fully dressed when he lies down on the chaise longue for his afternoon nap. Meanwhile, Katia and the children empty the larder and hide provisions all over the house. One never knows.

The master of the house prepares for the worst. As he lies there, his head is filled with images of revolutionary tribunals and executions. He notes: "If things are taken to extremes, it is not impossible that I will be shot for my behaviour during the war." And for a less extreme situation, he has already composed a few good lines. "I intend in such a case to say: listen, I am neither a Jew nor a war profiteer, nor any other despicable thing; I am a writer who built this house with the money earned from his intellectual work. I have 200 marks in my drawer: I will give it to you. Divide that between you rather than carving up my property and my books."

Thomas Mann was planning to speak to the revolutionaries as if they were a group of friendly (if anti-Semitic) tradesmen. Luckily for him, he was never forced to give his speech and offer up his small sum of money. What he said about the house was not entirely true, either: it had been purchased before the war by his mother-in-law, who was married to the rich Jewish mathematics professor Alfred Pringsheim. It made his relationship with her rather strained, especially since she didn't share his German-nationalist, pro-war, anti-democratic position in the slightest. She was horrified by the *Reflections of a Nonpolitical Man*, and when Katia told her about a positive review of the book in a Viennese daily newspaper, Hedwig Pringsheim retorted coolly: "Well, that's Vienna for you..."

What Thomas Mann meant by planning to tell the revolutionaries he was not a Jew is also not entirely clear. It was probably just self-evident to him that this assurance would protect him against all kinds of resentment. He himself was prone to anti-Semitic thoughts in these days, and he was sure that Munich, intellectual Munich, the majority of Munich, shared this fundamental aversion. "Both Munich and Bavaria, governed by Jewish scribblers. How long will the city put up with that?" he writes. The hatred will grow even greater over the days and weeks to come. Not against every Jew in the new government—he remains essentially well disposed towards Eisner—but Wilhelm Herzog attracts the full force of his rage, his disgust: "Our own co-regent a slimy literary racketeer like Herzog, who let himself be kept for years by a movie star, a moneymaker and profiteer at heart, with the big-city piss-elegance of the Jew boy, who would lunch only at the Odeon bar, but neglected to pay Ceconi's bill for partially patching up his sewer-grate teeth. That is the revolution! The ones involved are almost exclusively Jewish."

———

One of these Jews, a handsome, knowledge-hungry young man, had sat in Thomas Mann's house a year or so earlier, reciting his poems. They had met at a tavern to which Professor Arthur Kutscher, with whom the young man was studying German literature, regularly invited writers to give readings and meet his students. Thomas Mann had read there and the young student, who had been invalided out of military service at the start of 1916, took the opportunity to request a private audience with the man he so admired.

Now he is sitting here, Ernst Toller, the student, his pockets full of poems, drinking tea and not quite knowing when the proper moment would be to get them out. And read them, at long last. That, after all, is the reason he's here. What will Mann say? Will he acknowledge him as a kindred spirit? As a writer?

Ernst Toller, Jew, born in 1893 in the Province of Posen, had begun the war as an enthusiast, like everyone else. He had written:

> In the roaring storm, a curly-headed
> boy unfurls his limbs:
> Wake up, wake up, what was is dead;
> Wake to this new beginning.

And:

> Never so keenly have I felt
> My love for Germany
> As when springtime fills the air
> In the midst of the melee.

And more along the same lines. But now he has turned away from the war and started throwing himself into university, books, poetry, and he has almost finished his first play. He is brimming with faith in the power of words, poetry, drama. A poem written shortly before he was released from the war is entitled "New Year's Eve 1916":

> A ghastly, greenish visage now appears:
> Seize life, it tells me with a mirthless grin,
> Take courage boy, for I am the New Year!
> It thunders: Curse the god who let me in.

That afternoon in Thomas Mann's villa, he does finally venture to take out some poems. He reads and reads and Thomas Mann says: "Hm." Then nothing, then "Hm" again. What does that mean, asks the nervous Toller. Then Thomas Mann asks Toller to give him the pages, and they read through the lines together once more. He praises the things he likes, criticizes what he regards as vulgar, and when they have finished he asks the young man to leave the poems with him. Toller thanks him and leaves the villa on the Isar with a spring in his step.

A few days later he receives a long letter in which Thomas Mann gives more detailed praise and criticism, having taken a thorough look at the texts. Later in his autobiography *I Was a German*, Toller will write that the young man he was then "never forgot this extraordinary courtesy".

Ernst Toller is an open-hearted poet, a great admirer; he is looking for role models, guiding stars, people he can follow. He studies with great zeal, but before long, of course, that isn't enough for him. Germany is still fighting a war, and the war must end, the people must rise up and form an alliance:

the intellectuals and the people, the writers and the workers, the many and the few.

He goes to study in Heidelberg and attends a meeting of Germany's intellectuals at Castle Lauenstein, convened by the publisher Eugen Diedrichs, where the old and the young, professors and poets, Richard Dehmel and Max Weber, Werner Sombart and Walter von Molo have come together to talk about a new Germany. But they are so cautious, so old, so quiet. Ernst Toller listens, but he can't comprehend this muted opposition in the face of the war raging outside. He knows it's presumptuous of him to speak here, but speak he must. He calls out: "Show us the way! The days are burning and the nights too, we can't wait any longer!"

But where are the people who will lead Germany's youth? Toller writes to Gerhard Hauptmann: "We are waiting for a word from an intellectual leader we can believe in!" Hauptmann says nothing. In Munich, Toller sees Rainer Maria Rilke in a bookshop: "I haven't written any poetry for years," he tells the young man in a soft voice. "The war has struck me dumb."

Toller already knows that he must speak. That he has to take matters into his own hands. It was his admiration for all the greats, all the masters of words that made him look on despondently from the sidelines for so long.

But now he has had enough. In Heidelberg he starts a combat league, which he calls the "League of German Youth for Culture and Politics". He attracts no more than a few founding members. The league's guidelines are his own composition. "Love of the people forces us to take action," he writes. "We want to step forward and become leaders." "We do not want communities artificially fettered, our hearts clamped in a steel ring." The aims of the league, the aims of the fight

are absolute: "The elimination of poverty", "A peaceful solution to the contradictions of living as nations", "Harmony of
physical, spiritual and intellectual culture", "comprehensive
schools" and the cheap or free distribution of "recent literature
with real humanity", such as Tolstoy's *Resurrection* and *Under
Fire* by Henri Barbusse.

The league's writings do not escape the notice of those in
power, and Toller risks being redrafted into the army. But
Toller is a fighter now. And more importantly, he is a speaker.

The twenty-year-old poet Gustav Regler, born in Saarland,
received medals for bravery in the war, but when faced with
the true horror at the front found himself, like Toller, in a psychiatric hospital. During these days, he stops off in Heidelberg
with his Baltic lover Hanna, and watches his beloved lose
her composure when faced with this fiery young man, who
is standing on a little platform in the shadow of Heidelberg
Castle. She describes him as "a sort of prophet". He must
meet this man, she tells him. He, Gustav Regler, still has a
lot to learn.

Regler himself sees Toller as a kind of "oracle priest",
which he means disparagingly. Probably in part because his
girlfriend admires this man so much and turns red whenever
she talks about him. Toller calls out: "Wake up! Wake up!"
He criticizes the mothers who have let their sons go to war.
Criticizes the warmongering press. Criticizes the clerics, "the
most miserable scoundrels who ever walked the earth!". He
rages against the silence of the lambs: "Your silence is more
dreadful than the agonized screams of those brothers whose
eyes were burnt out with devilish flamethrowers". And who
is to be the leader? Whom should they believe, whom should
they follow, to whom should they entrust themselves? "Believe
in yourselves, if you don't believe in me!"

Regler stands there with Hanna below the red castle and marvels: "I was struck by the face that turned towards mine in the moonlight. It was big and white with eyes like those of an ancient owl, their gaze penetrating and then suddenly dreamy. The man was in the act of speaking and he did not stop on my account. 'I want to collect the embittered ones,' he said.

His gestures were those of a tired actor. He had the Jewish countenance, on which the fate of that persecuted race is imprinted like the traces of a secret malady."

Toller burns, Toller fights, Toller speaks. All the while fearing he will be called up again. His health, however, is not always good. His heart, his nerves—he is taken to hospital, then transferred to a specialist in Berlin, who sends him to a sanatorium in Grunewald. Numerous psychiatric evaluations testify that Toller suffers from a tremendous variety of nervous complaints. One calls him a "severe hysteric, with a pathological addiction to making himself interesting". Another sees him as a "neurasthenic with a very inflated sense of self", while a third doctor testifies that he has "a hysterical personality, leading to a disharmonious disposition, excitability and a tendency towards enthusiasm, uncritical acceptance, obstinacy and credulity when it comes to the idea he has currently latched on to".

He himself writes to the well-loved anarchist, literary scholar, Shakespeare researcher, Hölderlin reader, social reformer and radical pacifist Gustav Landauer about himself and his great aims: "I want to get under the skin of life, in whatever form it appears, I want to plough love into it, but I also want to overthrow everything that has become rigid, if I have to, for the sake of the human spirit." He demands that "those who walk with us" give their all. The mission life has handed to us: "As I understand it, you must come to an insight in its fullness through adversity, suffering, must have seen yourself 'uprooted', must have wagered your life and danced with death, must have suffered intellectually and overcome that suffering—must have struggled with humanity."

He knows how that will sound to someone who doesn't know him yet. To be on the safe side, he adds: "I am not a mystic, who only sees myself and God, and not the rest of humanity." No, his main focus is the new community—a nascent thing, in which he will play a decisive part—and for that reason he wants to use all the strength and power of the word to set people like the bearded guru Landauer in motion.

The same goes for Kurt Eisner, the other bearded guru he meets in Berlin at the start of 1918. Sanatorium or no, in Berlin Toller has read parts of his first play aloud to a circle of friends. At that point it was called *The Uprooted*; later it will be staged as *Transformation*. It is also the story of his own transformation, from a volunteer soldier into a pacifist, a man hoping for a new world, a rhetorician of the revolution. Toller himself described the play as a big political pamphlet, theatre as a means of agitation. The prologue is called "Shake-up", and it ends:

> A brother bore within him a strong will
> To build ecstatic temples to great joy
> And open wide the gates to suffering
> Ready to act.
> He hurled this hard and blazing cry:
> The way! The way!
> Thou poet, show us.

At the end of the play, everyone on stage joins hands and cries out:

Brothers, now raise up your tortured hands,
Sing out an end to persecution!
Rebellion shall stride through our free land,
Revolution! Revolution!

And that was what Toller read, in the sculptor Krone's gallery in Berlin's west end. The play and the dramatist made such an impression on his friends that they told Kurt Eisner about them, and he set off at once for the sanatorium in Grunewald to meet this young man. They see eye to eye immediately, talk about the persecution of the Heidelberg students, about poetry, theatre and politics. Eisner invites Toller to visit him in Munich, if he should ever find himself there.

And it won't be long before he does. Toller travels to Munich at the end of January; on the train he works on an appeal to the German people, which he will show to Kurt Eisner not long after he arrives. They meet in the Deutscher Kaiser restaurant, where Eisner always has lunch, and the following day Eisner invites him back to his apartment in Großhadern. Toller shows him his call to action and asks if it could be printed on a flyer; Eisner says no, it's not good enough. But he tells Toller to come to the Colosseum the following day, where he is going to give a speech, an important speech.

And Toller goes. It is a fantastic speech. Later, Eisner will say that these days in January were the best of his life. He has fought against the war alone for so long, and in these days he realizes he is not alone any longer. He talks about German war guilt, about the guilt of German industry. The police are present in great numbers, and "for that very reason" he speaks "with the greatest recklessness". The audience is electrified. One member in particular—Toller—is beside himself. "Once his speech was over I went up to Eisner. He must have seen how worked up I was and tried to calm me down. I myself did not take the floor; in my excitement I would never have been capable of it."

Ernst Toller is a young man who often gets carried away. Excitable, given to enthusiasm, he can be lifted off his feet by words. He is invited to the discussion evening at the Golden Anchor the following evening. He goes, listens, and this time is immediately disappointed by that day's nameless orator. A political speech constructed from syntactical building blocks, lifeless, dull. That can't be it. He pipes up. Might he be permitted to say a few words. Yes, he might. And he does.

Oskar Maria Graf is in the audience. He feels as if a storm has broken over him: "Fiery, ecstatic, gesticulating and grimacing wildly, he shouted out his feelings. He trembled as if feverish and foamed at the mouth.

He seemed quite black to me. Deep, dark eyes, thick black hair, handsome eyebrows and a rather sallow face.

'You mothers!' he cried out—again and again—as he painted the horrors of war with a poetical, rhetorical fire: 'You brothers and sisters!'

He carried everyone along with him. Here and there, women were weeping or growing quite agitated.

'Down with the war! Send Ludendorff to the gallows!' Everyone agreed."

Graf gets up and says he's glad someone is finally talking about universal human concerns, not party politics. And then he himself speaks about Tolstoy and his ideas on saving humanity, eliminating poverty and abolishing property. Then a party man speaks up and says all right, enough of the general "bluster". It's time to turn back to specific issues.

Graf and Toller take the tram home together. "Do you write, too?" Toller asks him eagerly. "Yes, all kinds of things," says Graf. Toller tells him about his first play, which is already being printed. He is accompanied by a petite blonde girlfriend who gazes at him all through the journey in mute admiration.

Over the next few days there are large gatherings on the Theresienwiese. The first of the mass strikes takes place, Kurt Eisner is arrested and imprisoned until October, and shortly afterwards Toller is taken into custody as well. He is charged with treason and calling for strikes. He spends three months in a military jail.

When Toller hears about Eisner's triumphal march through Munich, months later, he is in bed with a high fever at his mother's house in Landsberg. But no matter: he has to be there. He sends a telegram to Eisner, asking if he can help. He is ready to serve. Eisner sends a prompt, friendly reply, thanking the young man without really extending an invitation. But that's enough for Toller. He takes it to mean that he will be welcomed by the new Prime Minister, and travels to Munich. He has to be there. He is elected as the deputy chair of the "Executive Committee". Finally turning words into deeds. Toller is happy.

In a military hospital in Western Pomerania, the lance corporal and dispatch-runner Adolf Hitler is slowly regaining his eyesight. Almost a month earlier, he had nearly been blinded in an English mustard-gas attack on the front at Comines. It was the same place he had been positioned four years previously, when the Germans were on the attack and the mood was euphoric. Now the enemy was advancing, and Hitler delivered his last message. A small act of heroism before the world went dark for him, according to his own melodramatic description: "Towards morning the pain gripped me more fiercely from one quarter-hour to the next, and at about seven o'clock I staggered and stumbled back, my eyes burning, to deliver my last message of the war. Just a few hours later, my eyes were transformed into glowing coals, and I was plunged into darkness." The pale man with the thin face and the little moustache was taken first to the field hospital near Oudenaarde, and from there to the reserve hospital in Pasewalk near Stettin. Here he slowly regained his sight. Some researchers later claimed the blindness was caused not by mustard gas, but by the lance corporal's own hysterical reaction to the attack. In the Pasewalk hospital, they say, the psychiatrist Edmund Forster restored his vision using hypnosis—and then forgot to wake the patient from his trance. But that is mere speculation.

In any case, sailors with revolution in mind have also been turning up in Pasewalk since the start of November, though Hitler still believes it's a "more or less local matter". In *Mein Kampf* he will later write: "I could not imagine that the madness would break out in Munich as well. To me, loyalty to the honourable House of Wittelsbach still seemed stronger than the will of a few Jews."

But by 10th November, there is no more denying it. The pastor comes into the field hospital and gives the invalids news of the capitulation and the revolutions in Berlin and Munich. The horror almost makes Hitler go blind again: "As everything started to turn black once more, I groped my way back to the ward, threw myself down on my cot and buried my burning head in the blanket and pillows. I had not wept since the day I stood at my mother's graveside."

But in the memory presented for public consumption, the young man with the poor vision quickly pulls himself together again: "Then the voice of my conscience thundered out: you miserable baby, are you going to cry while thousands have it a hundred times worse than you?"

In the story of his "struggle", everything then happens very, very quickly. Lance Corporal Adolf Hitler, who in four years with his company had been notable only for his loyalty and obedience, claims that after hearing the fateful news he acquired a sudden decisiveness: "In the days that followed I became aware of my destiny. I now laughed when I thought of my own future, a future which just a short time before had caused me such bitter worry."

But for the time being he returns to his division, to his "ersatz family". Returns also to his friend Ernst Schmidt, a failed fine artist just like Hitler; the pair are currently almost inseparable. Within the regiment people whisper that the two men, neither of whom shows any interest in women, are a couple. The demobilization unit of the List Regiment, to which Hitler belongs, is stationed in Munich. Hitler has a deep aversion to Munich, but his one desire is to stay with his regiment. He has no career, no family, no money, no social connections. All he has is his unit, his comrades, his superiors, the army. He doesn't want to be demobilized, but he doesn't want to join the new volunteer forces known as Freikorps, either, as other demobilized German nationalists have done. Is Adolf Hitler, a man whom his superiors value for his unremarkable but unfailingly loyal execution of orders, already as filled with hatred for all Social Democrats, socialists and Jews as he later claims?

He is discharged from Pasewalk on 19th November and sets off alone for Munich to meet his unit, which will soon arrive from Belgium. He reaches Berlin on 20th November, alighting at the Stettiner Bahnhof. The train to Munich departs from the Anhalter Bahnhof. He could take the direct route along Friedrichstraße, but he doesn't, because a huge demonstration of socialist power is taking place outside the royal palace.

It could have been loathing and disgust that drove the lonely lance corporal to the palace square that day. But it might also have been—and much of Hitler's behaviour over the weeks to come also speaks for this—that he had not yet come to hate the new governments in Berlin and Munich. Yes, it even seems possible that he felt a magnetic pull from the red sea of people on this November day in Berlin, and that he was driven there by fascination. Even in *Mein Kampf*, this seems to shine through: "After the war I was then present at a mass rally for Marxism in front of the royal palace and in the Lustgarten. A sea of red flags, red scarves and red flowers gave this rally, in which around 120,000 people took part, a powerful appearance at least outwardly. I myself could feel and understand how easily a man of the people could fall prey to the suggestive charm of such a grandiose-looking spectacle."

In the months that follow he will have the opportunity to see plenty of other dramatic spectacles in the theatrical city of Munich. Hitler arrives. Hitler is Kurt Eisner's soldier.

A young dramatist has already written a play about the stirring events of these weeks. He has just turned twelve, on 18th November 1918; he reads a book a day, has thick, dark, tousled hair, dreamy eyes, often wears a sailor suit and spends most of his time with his sister Erika, who is a year older. He lives in that splendid villa we have already encountered. Everything he knows about politics comes from the grown-ups, from his parents, his politically indecisive father, his pro-democracy mother and his grandmother, who gave him Bertha von Suttner's pacifist novel *Lay Down Your Arms* for Christmas, an edition that had belonged to his great-grandmother Hedwig Dohm, one of Germany's first campaigners for women's rights.

"Revolution! Revolution! Revolution!" he writes in his diary. "Trucks full of soldiers speed through the streets; window panes are smashed; Kurt Eisner is President... It all sounds so fantastic, so incredible. And yet it is somehow flattering to imagine that people might later discuss our Bavarian Revolution with the same sort of seriousness we have when talking about Danton and Robespierre. Unfortunately, we could not attend the performance of the Magician Uferino. That was quite a disappointment but otherwise my birthday was a lot of fun. I now possess the complete works of Kleist and Grillparzer and Körner and Chamisso."

Klaus Mann finds it all very, very exciting. He loses no time in turning these events into a play, which he calls *Bavaria's Revolution*. A procrastinating, humanitarian Kurt Eisner is urged towards revolution and into power by the dogged rabble-rousers Wilhelm Herzog and Erich Mühsam. Herzog spurs on the hesitant man: "There is no greater good, the people are free! The red flag is flying, we are hailed as saviours and you, Eisner, are Prime Minister." To which Klaus Mann's Eisner replies: "I have a terrible fear that blood will be spilt." Herzog, a vampire of the revolution, drives him on. Eisner, trembling, says: "You make me shudder! But if it can be done without bloodshed, I should be very glad."

The imaginary Eisner, with his humanitarian sensibilities, doesn't have an easy time of it. Klaus Mann gives him a monologue: "But how beautiful I thought it to liberate a people, to deliver, to govern, to be a father to them! Those are lost illusions. I am challenged from all sides. Nothing is so hard as man's ingratitude! I stand on quaking feet."

Whether it was his feet that were quaking, or the ground beneath them—the boy in the sailor suit, the fiercely empathetic son of the great German writer Thomas Mann, described events exactly as they were.

The months that followed that November night when the revolutionaries suddenly seized power were a chaotic time. From the very beginning, Eisner was assailed by opponents from every political camp. Not just from the right—the nationalists, royalists, anti-Semites and anti-democrats. No, his most dangerous and unrelenting opponents were always the moderate left—the Bavarian Majority Social Democrats led by Erhard Auer; Friedrich Ebert and Gustav Noske from the ruling Social Democratic Party in Berlin—and the radical left, the anarchists and communists in Munich and Berlin.

In Eisner's first address to the new state parliament on 8th November, he introduces his new government: "In recent days we have shown that people can make history in the space of a few hours, and that revolutionaries can change things for all time. None of you, whatever your views, will today harbour the foolish belief that the line our peaceful uprising has drawn under everything that is past can ever be rubbed out. And anyone who has the impression that this radical overhaul of the Bavarian constitution, of life as a whole, has been somewhat anarchistic—well, that is simply a misunderstanding of the present moment."

Bavaria's new head of state, catapulted into power in the night by a revolutionary overthrow, apologizes for the temporary disorder. It is as if he wants to prove the claim in Thomas Mann's diary that every revolution becomes conservative at the very moment it is accomplished. Eisner also intends to leave the ministries largely untouched, as he announces to the surprised gentlemen in the Landtag. On this 8th November, the debating chamber is occupied by members of the Workers', Soldiers' and Peasants' Councils, members of the Social Democratic factions, the Peasants' League from the old parliament and a few liberal MPs. The reason for retaining the structure of the old ministries, as Eisner explains, is "that we do not want to make it any harder than necessary for the civil servants, on whose joyful, perhaps relieved support we are relying, and whose lot in this democracy will surely be quite different from what it was before, to find their feet in these new circumstances".

Then he introduces his cabinet and presents himself, to applause from the parliament, not only as the new government's Prime Minister but also as its Foreign Minister. He explains that the War Ministry will now be known as the Ministry for Military Affairs and headed by a civilian, Albert Roßhaupter from the SPD. When he introduces the Home Office Minister—"one of the most important offices, due to the provision of food supplies"—and names Erhard Auer, there is uproar.

But this is one of the core principles of Eisner's government. He wants to—he has to—collaborate with the more conservative Majority Social Democrats. His own party, the Independent Social Democrats (USPD), has very little structured support, particularly in more rural areas: not much of a base to build on in future elections. And Eisner wants to be the prime minister of as many Bavarians as possible. A prime minister for the people, that's his vision, that's his dream. And so he speaks directly to the anti-Auer contingent in the Landtag: "I hear protests and 'No'; but if we are determined henceforth to walk the path to social democracy and the nation of workers together, then this too is a symbol: the fact that we can recommend Herr Auer for this office with complete conviction." At this point, the Landtag stenographers record applause.

During those first days, Eisner is carried along on a wave of euphoria. Even he can't believe how easily everything has fallen into place. A thousand-year-old kingdom evaporating without any resistance. The ease of this sudden, final victory, after a four-year battle against superior opponents.

The first few days were a democratic carnival. The royal ministers cleared out their offices, and red flags hung on Munich's public buildings and the steeples of its cathedral, the Frauenkirche. Everywhere groups of people were deep in discussion; the whole city was on its feet. Thousand-strong crowds could often be seen on Stachus Square and on Marienplatz, there was a political street-preacher on every corner of the old town, trucks full of heavily armed revolutionaries passed by, and the streets teemed with beggars, their knapsacks and carts full of bottles and tins, sailors, soldiers with no insignia on their uniforms, drifters. Munich debated, Munich exhaled. Some people still weren't taking this new government completely seriously. But the end of the war, the start of a new age: *that* they took seriously, and you could sense it everywhere.

In these first few days, Kurt Eisner seemed to grow wings. He was seen many times driving through the streets of Munich in an open car, his hair blowing in the wind. Everyone wanted to see him, and he liked to be seen. He was euphoric, despite the heavy blow he had suffered on only his second day in government. His most significant friend and ally, the blind peasant leader Ludwig Gandorfer, who had marched through Munich with him on the evening of 7th November and been appointed head of the Peasants' Council, a man respected and recognized by Bavaria's peasants, the new government's most important link to the unknown, unrevolutionary land *out there*—on only the second day of the new age, this man had been travelling to a peasants' meeting in Lower Bavaria when his car had come off the road on a sharp bend outside Schleißheim, killing him. His brother Karl took his place, but he didn't have blind Ludwig's popularity.

And the rural areas and the rural population were a substantial problem—perhaps the greatest problem facing the new government. In these lean times, the state capital was more dependent than ever on the goodwill of the peasants and farmers out there, on the supply of food, milk, meat, vegetables from the Bavarian countryside. But the peasants weren't interested in the "government of the people" and its discussions in Munich. They were the people, too. And even during the war, as long as their sons weren't called up, they'd had no interest in so-called world events. Nor did they have any time for the Peasants' Council and other modern folderol. Might Ludwig Gandorfer have changed that? In some parts of the state, perhaps. But that dream ended on a bend in the road near Schleißheim.

Still, these are the first days of the new age. Eisner's euphoria is tremendous, despite the death of his blind friend. The 17th of November is the best, most splendid day of his brief reign.

The new government has invited the people to a celebration of the revolution in the National Theatre. The tickets have been allocated by ballot. The new ministers are distributed all around the auditorium—there is no VIP area. There are no military insignia to be seen, either. Just red sashes, red ribbons, red armbands. The famous villa architect Emanuel von Seidl has decorated the opera house for the occasion. The theatrical city of Munich celebrates itself and its new Prime Minister.

He has chosen Beethoven for the musical programme. The *Leonore* overtures. The conductor is Bruno Walter, of course,

Thomas Mann's best friend, who very recently trembled in fear of losing his money and his life. It is a perfect concert.

Afterwards the curtains part and Eisner appears, with his little spectacles, unkempt beard and high forehead. There is a thunderous swell of applause. The curtains close behind him. He pauses, he looks, he begins:

"Friends! The notes that have just pierced your souls painted a monstrous picture of a tyrannical madness: the world seems sunk in an abyss, shattered. Suddenly, out of the darkness and despair a trumpet sounds, heralding a new earth, a new humanity, a new freedom. That was how Beethoven saw the fate of the world. He carried his heart, heavy with longing, through the gloomy times in which he lived. The work of art we have just heard is a prophetic prediction of the reality we are now experiencing."

Kurt Eisner gets carried away and takes the whole auditorium with him. That evening in the National Theatre he lays out his dream, the utopia he wants to transform into reality—indeed, he thinks reality has already been transformed. He sees, and he wants everyone else to see, that overnight reality has miraculously taken on the character of his wildest dreams. "Friends!" he cries again. "What we are experiencing in these days is a fairy tale that has become reality."

And he remembers his late friend, "with whom I strode through the streets of Munich, arm in arm, on that wild afternoon and evening, on that day when this new freedom was forged". He describes himself and Gandorfer as an unlikely pair of twin heroes: "This collaboration between a simple writer, an intellectual worker from the city, and a gifted, brave, heroic peasant from the country: this is a sign, a symbol of the new democracy that is coming to Bavaria, to Germany, to the world."

You people of Bavaria, you are the seeds of a new world. Here, on a small scale, is something that will become all-encompassing. The people will form an "army of salvation". And a permanent democracy. "By democracy, we do not mean that every few years all citizens will exercise their right to vote and rule the world with new ministers and a new parliament. We have found a new form of revolution, and we are also trying to develop a new form of democracy. We want constant co-operation with everyone who works in the city and out on the land."

This was a fundamental principle of his programme for government. Permanent democracy. That was what the councils were for. The councils were islands of permanent, democratic co-operation, which would convey their decisions directly to the government representatives. Eisner wanted strong councils; he was certain that the longer this ancient democratic structure was tested, used and filled with life, the stronger it would grow. And he was prepared to have an elected parliament working in parallel with the councils. The Majority Social Democrats just wanted a proper parliament. The communists and anarchists, but also some sections of his own party, the USPD, just wanted the councils. Eisner believed there was a compromise. He believed councils and parliament could exist together; his belief in the people and their will to participate was so strong that he was sure the councils would win out all by themselves over time. In the end, parliament would become superfluous or dwindle into something that was just there for show, for form's sake. Eisner tells his audience that he has received thousands of letters in the last few days. Enthusiasm is stirring out there. He is carried away and he carries everyone with him. It is, so he proclaims to the high-ceilinged auditorium, "a shake-up of the most radical kind".

Permanent involvement in everything—this is the first principle of Eisner's rule. And then he comes to the second: peace. And the impossibility of anyone on German soil ever starting another war. He is convinced of the German Kaiser's war guilt. He pleads guilty on behalf of Germany—no, he cries out in liturgical fashion: "We confess our sins!" But then he limits this confession. It is not he, an opponent of the war from the very start, who is to blame, but the others, the rulers of old, the German monarchs. "By removing the people guilty of this heinous crime," he goes on—then corrects himself at once: "by forcing them aside more humanely than ever before, with a consideration they have not earned", the way has been cleared for everlasting peace. "That was the last war!" cries Eisner.

Then comes the finale of this ceremony to usher in the new Bavaria, the dream land of Kurt Eisner and his comrades: "We welcome those who were our enemies. We send our greetings to the people of France, Italy, England and America. We want to build this new age with them [...] Freedom lifts her head: follow her call!"

Cheering erupts, thunderous applause; the general desire to participate seems tangible to everyone in Munich's National Theatre that evening, particularly the speaker.

But that is soon over. When he repeats the same speech in the same place twelve days later for an audience of school and university students, catcalls and whistles shrill through the auditorium as soon as the *Leonore* overtures have finished. "Eat dirt!" they shout at Eisner, when he says he hasn't had a proper breakfast yet. And when he starts to talk about the "cursed state of the past", he is drowned out by furious whistling.

Kurt Eisner himself has almost entirely lost faith in his new empire. On 25th November he travelled to Berlin for the conference of German state prime ministers. But the main goal of his trip was to get the Berlin papers to publish secret documents that would prove Germany's war guilt. For this purpose, Eisner had requested reports for the months of July and August 1914 from the Bavarian Ambassador to Berlin. State Councillor Lößl had "stammered" that he'd destroyed some reports on 7th November, as he feared they might put certain people in danger. No matter: in Eisner's view, they still had sufficient evidence to prove quite clearly that in the weeks leading up to the outbreak of war, the German government had encouraged its Austrian allies to take action against Serbia. And now Eisner wanted to see those documents published.

With this move, the Bavarian Prime Minister hoped to achieve two things. First, he wanted to discredit the old nomenklatura in the German Foreign Ministry who were preparing for peace negotiations with the Entente. He held them to be the true guilty parties for fundamental aspects of the war, and he was certain that, with these people at the negotiating table, the victorious powers would impose punitive conditions on Germany in any peace agreement. And that was the second and most essential reason for his action. If he could force Germany to confess her guilt, her negotiating partners might be moved to agree a more commodious peace treaty. On the day of his National Theatre speech he had received a telegram from the United States, from one of President Wilson's intermediaries, which had strengthened Eisner's resolve. This intermediary, the theologian George Davis Herron, said he had spoken with Wilson and as a result of that conversation, "Above all I advise you urgently [...] to take the first steps towards a full and frank confession of the

German government's guilt and misdeeds at the start of the war, and of the cruelties with which the war was waged. The moral impact of such an attitude would be considerable," said the American.

That was Eisner's belief, too. And so he set out to force the German government into a confession of guilt.

The documents were to be published in all the country's major newspapers. Today it would probably be called Eisner-Leaks. But first, he had decided to give an exclusive to the *Berliner Tageblatt* and the *Vossische Zeitung*. The latter was Berlin's most influential daily paper and had been run by the legendary journalist Theodor Wolff since 1906.

The Prime Minister of Bavaria invited Wolff to the grand Bavarian embassy building in Berlin to hand over the documents and explain the motives behind his actions. But above all he wanted to tell the famous journalist about his home-grown revolution. "Our revolution was truly beautiful," he gushed to Theodor Wolff. "No blood was spilt, and it was a splendid piece of theatre; we all went out onto the streets and stormed the barracks." He also had some harsh words for Berlin's SPD-led government, which he said had earned no trust and had no sympathy abroad. Wolff explained to Eisner that he took a different view of things, and when Eisner saw that they weren't going to agree, he merely reiterated with a rather wistful, dreamy air: "You should have seen our revolution in Munich." As if he was adding inwardly, with a sigh: then you would understand me and believe in humanity and realize that glorious things can happen.

But Wolff didn't believe; he just published the documents as agreed, the day before all the other newspapers in the country.

Eisner was feeling downhearted after his meeting with Theodor Wolff. His encounter with the communist leader

Karl Liebknecht had hit him even harder. He had received Liebknecht in the Bavarian embassy a little earlier, expecting a few words of support for his Bavarian people's government. But Liebknecht had not the slightest intention of supporting him. He made it abundantly clear to Eisner that he didn't approve of his compromise regime in Bavaria at all. Socialism could only be introduced if everything else was first torn down. The country could only be built anew once the entire capitalist system had been destroyed.

This is what a disillusioned Eisner writes about the meeting in a file note following his Berlin visit. He knows that he will now have to contend with even more vehement opposition from the radical left in his sleepy southern state. And from the Majority Social Democrats, who are sharply criticizing his publication of the documents. Someone, probably Fechenbach, adds a brief comment underneath Eisner's note about his meeting with Liebknecht: "Eisner at home: the revolution has failed."

Already? Barely three weeks after Munich's night of dreams? Less than ten days after his triumph in the National Theatre?

Kurt Eisner had been deceived by the great surge on that night of 7th November. Power had just been hanging in the air; all he had to do was reach up and pluck it, all he had to do was keep marching when Auer and his friends had gone home. Had he really thought things could go on like that? Had he believed he could become a fêted people's king, the man everyone had been waiting for, the man who would bring the people a longed-for freedom, a longed-for reconciliation with their neighbours, who would bring democracy and be loved and celebrated for it? The longed-for realization of Schiller's and Beethoven's vision, less than 100 years after the completion of the Ninth Symphony: "I embrace you, O you millions! Here's a kiss for all the world!" Did Kurt Eisner really think people had just been waiting for this glorious moment like he had, and would now tread this path with him, too?

No, Eisner wasn't that naive. Of course he knew that the entire political system couldn't be overturned in a single night, and all its loose ends then tied up without any trouble. But the first days had been so easy. And he was drunk on his own great, beautiful words. His dream! Art: woken into life. Politics: constant, rigorous, good-willed debate and co-operation among equals. Reconciliation with everyone. Who on earth could object to that? And now everywhere he went he was beset by misgivings, resistance, scorn, mockery and increasingly naked hatred. Even those well-meaning people he'd thought were his political friends were turning against him.

New, radical left-wing movements were being founded in direct opposition to his government. His former comrade, the anarchist Erich Mühsam, started a "union of revolutionary internationalists". A Russian-German student from Moscow, Max Levien, founded the communist Spartacus League. The Social Democrats were pushing for quick elections, and his ministers started openly turning away from their leader.

Outwardly, Kurt Eisner remained unruffled. But these were bitter weeks. Where had the euphoria gone? How could he go on playing the proud Prime Minister, showing his people the way? He made frequent trips out into the countryside, to give speeches to the peasants, to drum up enthusiasm for the idea of active democracy and persuade those country-dwellers who had always had everything decided for them by people in cities that they should get involved.

But in rural Bavaria, interest was laughably sparse. Whatever happened, life would go on there just as it always had. The ideal government would be one that no one noticed out here. "But *we* are in government now!" the revolutionary poet Oskar Maria Graf shouted at a friend during one of these trips. "You?" the friend replied scornfully. "Well I'm sure you'll do all manner of clever things. But no one out here gives a fig!"

Graf, euphoric in the city, is instantly cooled to a realistic temperature by his return to the countryside. "There they go making wars and revolutions and running around and fighting, getting themselves shot dead for their dogmatic ideas, making laws, banning things and arresting people... And out here, everything takes its usual course: the farmer ploughs his fields, the corn grows, winter and summer come, people are born and die, and everything is peaceful and lovely... So what is all the fuss about?"

But then things stopped being quite so peaceful. When Eisner came and made speeches, he was subjected to attacks just as vicious as those in the city. There were plans and attempts made to abduct him and install the SPD's Erhard Auer as Prime Minister. Right-wing nationalists kept addressing Eisner as "Salomon Koshinski", which according to a persistent rumour in the anti-Semitic press was the Prime Minister's true, East Galician name. As much as he put on a Bavarian accent and emphasized his love for the state, the Berlin Jew Eisner had a very difficult time in the rural parts of Bavaria. More bluntly: he didn't stand a chance.

And the assaults from the Bavarian press in the city were getting increasingly aggressive. On 6th December Kurt Eisner summoned the editor-in-chief of the *Bayerische Kurier* to his office, to complain about numerous errors in the paper's reports, including the spreading of the "Koshinski" rumour. The conversation was reasonable and businesslike, but then the editor-in-chief warned him against an impending occupation of his editorial offices and printing press. Eisner assured him there was nothing to fear. But as the gentleman from the *Kurier* turned to leave, a message reached the ministry that the paper's building was being stormed.

Erich Mühsam and some of his comrades had occupied the offices and the press, declaring that the business had been socialized and the workers were now partners. The very next morning, the front page of the *Bayerische Kurier* carried a call to action addressed to the "revolutionary internationalists of Bavaria", starting with the announcement: "Brothers! Tonight, the soldiers and workers of Munich have seized control of the newspapers."

The Prime Minister appeared in person at the paper's offices the same morning and had Mühsam and his friends forcibly ejected with the help of armed guards. Eisner instructed that the paper was to resume operating as it had before the occupation. But the printers weren't exactly happy to be relieved of their new ownership so soon. One of them turned directly to Kurt Eisner: "Oh yes, Prime Minister? And woss 'appening about socialization?"

Nothing had happened about socialization. And nothing else was socialized during these days in Munich, either.

But Erich Mühsam and his troops had scarcely been thrown out of the print shop before they moved on to the next target: Erhard Auer's apartment. On 2nd December he had publicly threatened to resign as Minister of the Interior if Eisner didn't hurry up and announce a date for elections to the Landtag. Under the increasing pressure, Eisner had finally fixed a date. But Mühsam and his revolutionary internationalists preferred Auer's resignation over an election date. And so they broke into his apartment. Auer would later speak of 300 armed men, though this is probably something of an exaggeration. In any case, Auer at once wrote a memo saying that, under the threat of violence, he had agreed to step down from his role as Minister of the Interior. The group was satisfied, took the declaration and left the minister's apartment. A short while later, however, they returned and informed Auer that the declaration wasn't good enough; he would have to leave out the part about violence and explain that he was stepping down voluntarily.

The jubilant crowd moved on to the Foreign Ministry, where they found the Prime Minister and told him of their fantastic triumph: the resignation of his arch-enemy. Eisner turned to the people he had thought were his friends and said: "Why didn't you tell me what you were planning? If you had asked me, I would probably have advised you against it. I'm sure it was well meant and done out of devotion to me, but it was not good. If you have any more complaints, any misgivings about the government, then bring them to me. I am always available to each and every one of you. And now, please, go home." A prime minister from the dream realm of friendship.

A teacher, intellectual and arch-reactionary member of the Munich bourgeoisie, Josef Hofmiller, commented on this brief address in his diary, noting in particular Eisner's use of the little word "probably", which was either clumsy or truly alarming: "'Probably' is a word one must never use when addressing crucial points. The SPD will not forgive him for this 'probably', and nor will the USPD." Finally, he wondered: "Does Eisner himself know what he wants? Even worse: does he in fact want anything? Or is he still just drifting? But he is not drifting alone, we are all with him: where are we drifting to?"

———

For the moment, they are drifting towards an election. It is planned for 12th January. The euphoria in the city has died down and there is a new, weary, irritable mood in the air. The battles between the different parties are becoming ever fiercer, ever more brutal; the government has long since ceased to be a unity government. Eisner's dream of uniting the left under his leadership has become a disaster.

On 7th January there is another demonstration on the Theresienwiese, with 4,000 unemployed people calling for a rise in unemployment support. The Minister for Social Affairs, Hans Unterleitner, addresses their demands, but they still set off for the ministry to demonstrate their strength and power. There are violent clashes with the police that leave three people dead and eight injured. Eisner is forced to arrest a few of the radical left-wing leaders, including his former comrade Erich Mühsam and the Russian-German student Max Levien, one of the founders of the German Communist Party.

So soon before the elections, there could not have been a more dramatic display of the split in the left. The ex-prisoner Eisner had his friend, the ex-prisoner Mühsam, thrown back in jail. The communists hated him for it. It was already some time since Eisner had been able to gain any more ground with the right and the Majority Social Democrats. The crack into which he fell shortly after taking power was getting steadily broader and deeper. And now the Prime Minister was practically alone there.

Mühsam and Levien's comrades of course refused to accept such a humiliation from this weak leader. They gathered outside the Foreign Ministry, where Eisner was currently residing, and demanded the prisoners be released to them. Eisner wouldn't grant them an audience, refused even to talk to a spokesman for the group. But the sailor Rudolf

Egelhofer, who would go on to lead Bavaria's Red Army, fetched a ladder and simply climbed in through Eisner's office window. Eisner then gave his consent to the prisoners' immediate release.

He later explained his capitulation to the Social Democrats by saying: "The sailors arrived armed with hand grenades. I didn't want murder outside my ministry, so at the last moment I gave in."

A political drama in the street. Each new day might bring another surprise. The more humorously minded inhabitants of Bavaria's capital city now regarded Eisner's rule as a comedy.

The popular actress Tilla Durieux, who has hardly missed a single political gathering during these days and visits the Foreign Ministry so often that Minister von Frauendorfer has described Eisner's official residence as a "bordello" and begun to spread rumours that the Prime Minister is having an affair with the actress—Tilla Durieux, then—is intending to pay the Prime Minister a visit that evening and, seeing the climbing sailor on the outside of the building, thinks it's Erich Mühsam. She looks. She marvels. She laughs. "We enjoyed the spectacle," she writes in her memoirs.

Politics—a spectacle. And a high art. In one of his first articles, written in 1888, Kurt Eisner himself had called for the socialization of the theatre. Had wanted the theatre to become a place of public instruction, of political education, where mankind could strive to become the best it could be. Now it is time to realize this vision. In a speech to the provisional National Council on 3rd January 1919, he reminds the audience of his earlier writing and castigates modern theatre. He rages against "the vulgarization of popular tastes", calls on the press not to write about any form of kitsch, operetta or cabaret and to discuss only true, great art. From now on, he wants critics to avoid "the very mention of any non-literary work". "I consider the theatre at present not to be a particularly substantial phenomenon," the former theatre critic, now Prime Minister, explains to the assembled parliamentarians. He recalls the theatre in Berlin during the war years: "Anyone who saw the war profiteers—who are recognizable at a glance—" (here the transcript states: "general mirth"), "making fun of tragedies, cackling at things they didn't understand, must surely regard these theatres as sites of fornication" (shouts of "very true!"), "as intellectual brothels for war profiteers."

He has a kind of private vision of utopia, he says: "I wish that I could write plays myself, to be staged as propaganda for our revolutionary politics, and that they could be taken out and performed in the most far-flung villages—then, through art, we would have the strongest, the mightiest means of educating people. I have spoken of *myself* [...] though what I really wanted to say was that I wish *you* could do this work."

A German prime minister wishes his country's parliamentarians could write plays to educate the populace. In this remarkable speech, he says his great aim is to "reinspire the people".

It is a speech made from the heart. You can sense immediately that this is everything to him. This is right at the core of his rule. This is art as a means of improving people. World art. He says that every true artist has to be an anarchist. That every true artist, every true writer must write at the risk of his life, otherwise what he creates will be worthless. Eisner contemplates the idea that significant writers should draw a salary from the state. He deplores the fact that literary historians on a fat salary dissect the work of starving writers. And wishes it were the other way around.

His state is an artists' state, creating opportunities, turning opportunities into realities. This is the core of the work, as the Bavarian Prime Minister Kurt Eisner understands it: "Politics is as much an art as painting pictures or composing string quartets. The medium of this political art, the material with which this political art seeks to prove itself, is society, the state, the people. I would therefore like to believe that a real statesman, a real government should have no stronger and more intimate connection than that with artists—their colleagues."

Yes, yes, he knows that a German statesman suspected of being able to write a poem is also suspected of having no idea about politics. But that is a purely German quirk. The world has long held a different view on this matter and soon so will people here, in Bavaria.

And then they will be in the vanguard of a global development, if Eisner has his way. Art will become the essential force for elevating and educating the masses. A utopia for which, as Eisner sees it, true, great art has long been striving: writing towards it, composing towards it. Beethoven's vision must be realized. And that is why he—his government—took power.

Eisner closes his speech on the role of art with a summary of his world view: "If we internationalize this question, if art is put into the service of the people everywhere, great art, then a new age will dawn for the future life of the nations, too. The problem our classical artists saw was how mankind could achieve freedom through beauty. Today, the problem is achieving beauty through freedom." Here, at the end of the speech, the stenographer records "lively applause".

Nine days later, the whole city was a stage. The Landtag elections. A chance for the people to endorse the revolution. Kurt

Eisner hadn't wanted elections. He suspected it was still too early for him and his party, the USPD. He knew that so far, very little had been achieved. He hadn't had time. Not enough time to take a new, permanent democratic state from zero to sixty, with this war-weary populace who had no experience of politics whatsoever. With these opponents on all sides. In this thin-skinned age. But he hadn't been able to put it off any longer. Auer and the other Majority Social Democrats had threatened to resign, leaving him without a government. A king with no ministers. A ridiculous figure.

Elections, then. The whole city was on its feet, in its Sunday best, dressed for the new democracy. For the first time, women were allowed to vote—and they voted in great numbers. A few men tried to cast a vote for a wife who had stayed at home but were told it wasn't allowed. Electoral law. Everyone had to vote for themselves, or not at all. Oh. People were slightly put out. Strange thing, this democracy. But all right, if those are the rules...

And then the results were out. The figures were a horror. A hurricane. Political reality had swept through the artists' government, and now it was gone. Pulverized. A dream. A joke. Eisner's vision of a government of the people had proven to be a fiction. The brainchild of an artist, born on a night when suddenly everything seemed possible. He wasn't a people's king at all. He wasn't carrying out the will of the Bavarian people.

Only 2.5 per cent of voters had chosen Eisner's USPD; 2.5 per cent voted for the party of the current head of government, a good two months after he had taken office. A disastrous result, probably unmatched anywhere in the world. And made even worse by the triumph of his arch-enemy Erhard Auer's party. The SPD had won 33 per cent of the vote, outdone only by the conservative Bavarian People's Party, with 35 per cent. The newly founded German Communist Party, the KPD, had decided to boycott the elections and hadn't put up any candidates. Of the 180 parliamentary seats that would make up the new Landtag, Eisner's party had won three. Three out of 180.

It was a shattering defeat. But also mildly liberating. The election in Rhineland-Pfalz had been delayed and wouldn't take place until the start of February, and only then would the final result of the Bavarian parliamentary elections be announced. The Landtag would meet for the first time on 21st February, and that was when Kurt Eisner would announce his resignation. Until then he was free. The battle was lost, but he was still Prime Minister.

He travels to Bern, to the International Socialist Conference. It is the first time the brothers from the opposing sides have come together for a congress since the end of the world war. Current and former warmongers and pacifists come face to face. Try to find a common language again. A common goal. A common enemy. But the atmosphere has been poisoned for good.

Eisner makes a speech. And Eisner doesn't want to forget. He doesn't want to forget how the Majority Social Democrats welcomed and backed the war. "It was a very peculiar error by our friends from the Majority, and it betrays an incredible lack of psychology that one must first wage war, wade through blood, engage in all those acts of German terrorism, before being able to offer a hand of friendship, with the words: enough now; let's make peace."

No, this is not a path to reconciliation with the Majority Social Democrats. Eisner calls for unity. But the pain is deep-seated. The ridicule, the attacks to which he was subjected for four and a half years. And above all the pain of knowing that once again, he has lost. Once again, he is fighting with a tiny minority on his side. When will history, when will the people finally concede that he's right? He is not deterred. "The fact that they have twelve million voters behind them does not mean their policies are good. The truth is not a multiplication sum."

But democracy is a majority decision. It's so difficult to accept that. It's so difficult to shake hands with those who are always in the majority. "We don't want to sully ourselves by judging these sinners. We are too proud to be their judges."

That doesn't sound like reconciliation. It sounds like stubbornness and disdain. And the will to carry on. He still wants his revolutionary Bavaria to set an example to the whole world. He calls out to the delegates: "Today, we are the world's most radical realm. We are not a democracy in name only; we are working to educate the entire population into participating, for we stand on the threshold of a socialist regime."

And he ends his polemic by saying: "We no longer have the patience to defer our dreams of socialism to some far-off time: we live today, and we want to act today. Let us act!"

Eisner's speech was a triumph. He was the star of the German delegation. The international delegates, particularly the Swiss, were impressed by his fire. And even more impressed by his admission of guilt. "It is clear today that this war was started by a small, crazed mob of Prussian soldiers in Germany," he shouted.

In the audience was a writer from Munich in her late forties. Her father was a garden architect and an illegitimate son of the Wittelsbach family, her mother a pianist from Paris. It is Annette Kolb, whose anti-war speech in Dresden in 1915 had caused uproar, and whom the Bavarian War Ministry had issued with a ban on travel and correspondence in 1916 for her "pacifist activities". She had spent the final years of the war in Swiss exile. Now she was sitting in the audience here and was shaken to the core.

"Never had we seen anyone grow beyond himself as Eisner did now. The spirit was on him so literally that his person now occupied the platform like nothing more than an abandoned shadow."

She sees a man enraptured, the spirit of his words almost transforming him into a spirit himself. She sees a new Jesus: "We held our breath. Before us stood a member of that band of silent martyrs who sacrificed themselves for the ideas of non-violence, truth and love of one's fellow man. This was their lot now, just as it was two thousand years ago."

Annette Kolb had seen a vanishing saint. In Germany, the papers spoke of a crazed, traitorous Jew, a lunatic who had been voted out but still nominally held office, going abroad and claiming that Germany alone was to blame for the war; wanting to put German prisoners of war to work in France. His speech had actually referred to "volunteers", but most of the papers failed to make this subtle distinction. The hatred for this man who had obtained the office of Prime Minister through lies and deception, and who, despite the terrible election debacle, was still travelling the world as Prime Minister and giving anti-German speeches—this hatred could hardly be surpassed.

He takes the train back to Munich, stopping in Basel to give another speech. Then he is back in his city, his state. His dream of a separate peace agreement between Bavaria and France, which could be a model for the whole of Germany, has foundered. France's Foreign Minister, Georges Clemenceau, has never taken Eisner or Bavaria's revolutionary government seriously. He prefers to negotiate with the elites in Berlin, men whom Eisner would call war criminals. And that, alongside the disastrous election result, is the greatest disappointment of Eisner's rule. The fact that, for all his fervent hopes of reconciliation, his willingness to take all the blame for the war and to make amends, he didn't manage to negotiate a good peace settlement with France. A peace that would be tolerable for Bavaria and Germany, with tolerable conditions. A hard peace, with the victorious powers making impossible demands, is something he fears just as much as his enemies in Berlin do.

Back in Munich, Eisner learns that Erhard Auer has already put together a new cabinet list for his future government. Eisner's name isn't on it. Is he still planning to play an active role in politics, his arch-enemy asks the current Prime Minister. He could envisage a role for him as Bavarian Ambassador to Prague. Eisner just smiles quietly.

But Auer's SPD won't be able to rule alone. And during the preliminary discussions on forming a coalition, the leader of the conservative Bavarian People's Party has demanded that Eisner be given a ministerial post in any future government. It is important to involve all the forces in society, they say. Eisner never learns of the conservatives' demand: Auer doesn't tell him.

On 13th February, Kurt Eisner gives another speech at the scene of his former triumph in the National Theatre. He speaks of the euphoria in Switzerland, the international socialists' willingness to reconcile and rebuild, now, at once, together.

But this time he takes to the stage as a beaten man, a man who can't understand the hatred he is reaping where he thought he had sowed only love, who can't comprehend his defeat and therefore elevates it to the greatest possible height. It isn't just Annette Kolb in Switzerland who has seen him as a kind of Jesus. It's also how he views himself. A new Jesus. The cross is ready and waiting for him. "Coming from Switzerland, back to the land of the first German Revolution, and becoming aware of the noise, the clamour of the press, the wild sedition among the people, one is reminded of ancient times, when men were crucified, and the words come to one's mind: 'They know not what they do.'"

Kurt Eisner senses what is to come. The hate, the bloodlust: none of it is a figment of his imagination. Shortly before his speech, someone slipped him a note. A call for "all fellow students, who fought in the war" to gather for a speech by that man who, in Switzerland, spoke "against the release of our fellow students who were taken prisoner". It ends with a literary quotation: "'Be swift, Governor, your time has run out!' Schiller: *Wilhelm Tell*."

Eisner reads the flyer aloud. And comments: "This is a call for murder. The 'governor' in this quotation is Governor Gessler. They are quite plainly calling for someone to murder me."

Perhaps Kurt Eisner hopes to allay the power of these words, to allay the evil magic, to scare off the lurking murderers, with the dazzling light in which his speech will bathe them.

A man is listening in the darkened auditorium. He has just arrived from Berlin, having been told that in Munich there is still "a crowd of moths like you round the political flame". He came straight from the station across the Rathausplatz to the Opera. He is the young writer Gustav Regler, whose lover had almost fainted at the sight of the fiery Toller speaking in Heidelberg. Now it's his turn to be enchanted.

He stands in a corner, people packed tightly around him, and listens in. "This is a time for reconciliation!" he hears, and: "It's time for goodness!" and: "From now on we must do nothing but build!"

The people around him start to shout out. A few of them are weeping. Is this hypnosis? The sceptic of Heidelberg sees, he hears, he feels, he marvels:

> The applause was now a tempest, and the man walked smiling through it; it was a Red Sea that he himself had caused to part.
>
> Suddenly a man sprang at him. The onlookers, fearing an assault, flung themselves upon this stranger, but the speaker stood protectively over him as he fell to the floor. "No one is to touch him!" I heard him say. "He can only be misguided." He bent down, raised the man to his feet and walked out with him arm in arm.
>
> It was a very convincing gesture. Perhaps everything is different here in the south, I thought [...] Perhaps only in certain climates were the true prophets born.

Yes. Perhaps everything is different in the south. Gustav Regler has witnessed a mystery play. The performance of an Act of the Saints. One of the Bavarian Prime Minister's final appearances. Another would follow three days later: a grotesque; an absurd comedy.

The Revolutionary Workers' Council has organized a demonstration on the Theresienwiese. They want people to call for the dismissal of ministers Auer and Roßhaupter, and for the occupation of newspaper offices and the university. Eisner tries to stop the demonstration. When he is forced to admit that he can't, he simply decides to put himself at the front of the procession. He rides ahead of the crowd in an open-topped car. But the ovations he was hoping for do not materialize. He has placed himself at the head of a demonstration against his own government, which has already been voted out. On the placards, he sees: "Don't be governed by a fool: the councils let the people rule!"

Erich Mühsam, who has called for this protest rally himself, describes Eisner riding in a car "at the head of a march that protested his own politics. [He] felt so out of place that he left halfway through the demonstration and joined the ministers Unterleitner and Jaffé, who awaited the delegation of the masses in the German Theatre. There, Landauer, as the delegation's speaker, presented the proletariat's demands."

Afterwards, the people walked on through the city with their banners and red flags, past the War Ministry—where they shouted: "Down with Roßhaupter!"—and back to the Theresienwiese. There was talk of setting off again for Eisner's ministry, since they weren't satisfied with the promises he had made outside the theatre. But then they abandoned the idea and went home. It was late and starting to get dark.

The whole spectacle is also witnessed by a young German aristocrat, a law student and lieutenant in the Bavarian Lifeguards Regiment, the son of Maximilian, Count von Arco auf Valley and his wife Emmy, Baroness von Oppenheim. This young man had been very keen to join the German nationalist Thule Society, but was denied membership on account of his mother's Jewish heritage. He sees this Prime Minister demonstrating against his own government, and he sees a lance corporal (still wearing a lance corporal's buttons on his uniform) being hit in the face by the demonstrators. He manages to get himself to safety just in time; a less agile sergeant who has been walking with him is dragged in and beaten up.

Anton, Count von Arco auf Valley has a revolver in his pocket. He is gripped by "a crazed anger towards Eisner", as he will later recall, "because he wanted to betray the Free State of Bavaria to the Spartacists, the Free State that the people had toiled and suffered to create. I would have liked to fly at Eisner there and then and pull the trigger. But that day I was held back by circumstance: the crowds were all around, and it would have been an unpropitious moment."

Five days later, there are no crowds to protect Eisner. The young aristocrat will be ready. The revolver is loaded.

Kurt Eisner writes his resignation speech. A rather dry summary; civil servants have put together the essential points for him: "the need to raise the salaries of public employees", "housing shortages", "unemployment benefits", "state budget plan", "necessary measures", and suchlike. He wants to say: but I worked hard. Why keep harping on about revolution and disorder and chaos and carnival and treason? In times of bitter defeat and disorientation he has led a functioning government, organized a proper election in a very short space of time, lost that election, and now here he is stepping down. It *has* been a dream. But this dream has involved a lot of work, and effort, often late into the night. He has worked at this dream, not just dreamt it. And if for all one's love and goodwill, one receives no love in return, then at least there should be something like—recognition? "Never," Kurt Eisner writes in his resignation speech, "never has a government conducted affairs of state under such difficult circumstances. But perhaps for that very reason it was spurred on by an unshakeable belief in the power of intellectual influence." And once again, he writes about the thing that has been most important to him in his short period of rule after the Great War, writes of his aim "to have a moral influence on the peoples of the world", and to lay the foundations for a new peace. "Only a policy of unconditional honesty, of bold openness and mutual trust leads to that peace for which downtrodden humanity pines." This is what he intends to say in his final speech as Prime Minister, to the members of parliament, the ministers, the audience in the gallery. And to the people out there, his Bavarian people, his subjects.

Many of these subjects had wavered as they watched the events of the past few months. Had been euphoric, disbelieving, believing. Rilke had feared, hoped, watched and listened with them in the beer halls. Had written: "I am one of the boys who takes the confidence of this new beginning (in which, let us be humble above all) to be their right and their (secret jubilation)."

But Rainer Maria Rilke, once enflamed in the beer halls, seems to have cooled off instantly in the reality that followed the revolution. Disappointed. He had even invited them to his rooms in Ainmillerstraße: the revolutionaries, the bringers of hope. Perhaps that was when he realized: we don't understand each other. All of you, you have in mind something different from me. Renewal, yes. The overturning of all values. Yes, but...

Oskar Maria Graf, the berserker poet who harboured an almost tender love for Rilke, described the meeting of the revolutionaries at Rilke's home:

To his studio apartment in Ainmillerstraße came active revolutionaries like Toller or the Communist Kurella and his young friends, and writers and bourgeois men whose intentions with the revolution were noble... They worried over the causes of the German collapse, our portion of war guilt and what the future might look like in Germany, and they were probably hoping that R. would take a useful position on it all. But the conversations were fruitless and did not satisfy them.

Graf goes on:

> He listened to his visitors without prejudice, but the things he said were entirely foreign to them... Curiously, however, something held them back from contradicting him. It occurred to me that most people preferred listening to R. over speaking with him, though he was anything but talkative. He had a very well-tempered voice, a soft, pleasant tone, and he spoke... with a deeply hidden shyness, an extreme nervous dread of banality and with the caution of a person who does not want to hurt anyone.

Rilke's letters in these weeks after the revolution, the weeks following his initial enthusiasm, are mournful and gloomy. A monstrous hangover after a little spree. "I confess that at first, I myself may have felt a certain swift and joyous confidence at the overthrow, for ever since I have been able to think, I have desired nothing so much for humankind as that it may at some point be empowered to open up an entirely new future, into which the whole sum of its calamitous past mistakes need not be carried over. It seemed to me that the revolution was just such a moment." But then he sees only dilettantism and obstinacy everywhere, "no youth", "no convincing fire". Perhaps the timing wasn't right, perhaps people are simply too exhausted?

On New Year's Eve, Rilke starts reading Oswald Spengler's *The Decline of the West* and is completely captivated by it. He recommends the book to all his female correspondents, sends a copy to Lou Andreas-Salomé. This brutally reactionary narrative of decline, the first volume of which has just been published, begins its triumphal march through the country's educated classes. It is an assessment of the Western spirit that sees the world and history as we know it coming to an end. Downfall, humility and exhaustion are everywhere. Greatness is a thing of the past. "The European academy combats self-annihilation by refining the intellect," Spengler writes. "Two centuries of civilization and orgies of scholarship—then one is sated. Not the individual, the soul of culture is sated... It is a general symptom. Since Lysipp there has been no great sculptor whose coming changed the world; after Rembrandt and Velázquez no painter; after Beethoven no musician. We would do well to heed why Goethe called himself a dilettante in comparison to Shakespeare, and why Nietzsche denied Wagner the title of Musician. What was the writing of tragedies or physics in Caesar's time?"

The arts, the sciences—we are all on the way out, according to Spengler. Perhaps the great Faustian thunderclap will deliver us. Perhaps—and this is only described in detail in the second volume, published in 1922, but it is sketched out in the first volume for anyone who can read—perhaps a new Caesar will come. The embodiment of the will to power that Nietzsche hoped for. One great, redeeming figure. Spengler is confident that this figure will soon deliver Germany and the West from weariness, from refinement, from decadence. "Always in history," he writes at the end of the second volume, "it is life and life only, race and the triumph of the will to power that count, not the victory of truths, inventions or money. World history is a courtroom: it has always found in favour of the stronger, fuller, more self-assured life, and granted it the right to exist... and condemned to death the people and nations for whom truth was more important than deeds, and justice more essential than power." The new "Caesarism", Spengler claims, is close at hand. There will be no resisting it. It will simply come, like the courtroom of history. Spengler is just its prophet: "We do not have the freedom to achieve this or that; we may do that which is necessary, or nothing." And he ends: "*Ducunt fata volentem, nolentem trahunt.*" In English: "Fate leads the willing and drags the unwilling."

Thomas Mann, who began reading the book just after Rilke, was completely fascinated and delighted by it. This book would be as epoch-making in his life as his reading of Schopenhauer once was. Later, having completely changed his political views, he would write that he had to force himself to take his eyes off the book, "so that I did not have to love it". Yes, Oswald Spengler's seductive story of decline had many people under its spell.

The German historical philosopher also commented on the events of November 1918 in his own unique style, writing to a friend that he is so consumed by "disgust and shame at the disgraceful events of recent times" that he sometimes thinks he "cannot survive it". These have been "weeks of the deepest ignominy that ever a nation has lived through", when everything "signifying German honour and dignity was dragged through the dirt by its enemies within and its enemies without".

Having regained his strength and—he may have been thinking of history's courtroom—some time after the fact, he did however add: "Today I can consider these events a little more calmly. In the revolution, I see something that could be useful to us, if those who are candidates for shaping our future know how to use it. Like any revolution, it was precipitated by the circles that will become its victims... I see that the German Revolution is taking the typical course: a slow dismantling of the existing order, then overthrow, wild radicalism, reversal."

Yes, he saw it. Overthrow, radicalism, reversal. And the victims who called for the revolution. But Kurt Eisner has not yet set off for the Landtag to give his resignation speech. Count Arco has not yet fired a shot.

Rilke is still reading Spengler in his writer's studio in Schwabing. At the start of 1919, he suddenly gives up all his social engagements. He rearranges his study, placing the desk and lectern in the middle of the floor. He writes to a female friend: "You will be amazed, I have changed my life, although I cannot say much of it yet."

He has changed his life. In early February of the year 1919, a countess writes him a letter, enclosing a picture of her three sons. Her sons are the twins Berthold and Alexander, and their younger brother Claus. The surname of this mother and her sons is von Stauffenberg. Rilke contemplates the photograph of the sons and writes to the mother: "I understand now the concerns you expressed." He adds: "Who knows whether it may not fall to us to overcome the greatest confusion and danger, so that the coming generation will grow up as it were naturally in a world that is very much renewed. For surely beyond the watershed of the war, for all its appalling height, the course of the river must flow easily into the new and the open."

Berthold: this is the young man to whom, six years later, the German poet Stefan George will dedicate a volume of poetry containing a poem entitled "Secret Germany". And Claus Schenk, Count von Stauffenberg, will be court-martialled and shot for trying to murder a German tyrant, a self-proclaimed German Caesar.

Lance Corporal Adolf Hitler is also back in Munich. He has been in Traunstein with his friend Ernst Schmidt, to whom he is still very close, guarding a camp of Russian prisoners of war. The people chosen for this task were not exactly the crème de la crème of the German military. But at least Schmidt and Hitler gave their commanding officers no cause for complaint. They are still the perfect unobtrusive subordinates. And they are still making no attempt to get themselves demobilized. The military is their home. Their family. The fact that they are now subjects of Eisner's revolutionary government does not upset them.

Adolf Hitler will later explain in *Mein Kampf* that he only returned to Munich in March 1919. Probably to disguise the fact that, in February, he took part in the greatest funeral procession Munich had ever seen. At least, a photo of the day shows a man who is the spitting image of him.

But no one is in mourning yet. The city and its population are still wavering between hatred and weariness, between hope and disappointment. Is it really all over so soon? Was the awakening, the hope, just the illusion of a single night?

"This whole revolution is nothing," Oskar Maria Graf grumbles. "They made a bit of a row for a single day, and now! What are they doing now?... Now they are starting another clean-up, and there is nothing there to clean up!"

Like many others who marched with the crowd on that November night, Graf is disappointed. Why have the wealthy not been dispossessed? Why is there no revolutionary council in session at all hours of the day and night? Why is everything continuing to take its course? Why was this Kurt Eisner placed in the prime minister's seat? "That's how the German Revolution is," he complains in conversation with his artist friend Schorsch. "As soon as you mean to begin, along come our lords and masters with soldiers, and if you don't obey they shoot! Very nice, that is!" And in his later memoir, *Prisoners All*, he continues: "I cursed the whole thing, lock, stock and barrel. I was unhappy and morose. This Munich revolution was a mere amusement to its opponents. It was dull, it was harmless, it was intolerable. It was a joke, and a bad one at that."

Graf continues going out to the Dutchman's house. There is drinking, carousing, laughter, and politics seems to have been forgotten. But it is still bubbling away inside him. He *does* want to change everything. He wants to dispossess the rich and enjoy their carefree existence at the same time. He wants a good life, for himself and for everyone else. But it's winter in Munich. Cold and grey. Graf walks the city streets. He is straight-talking, honest, canny, he gets into conversation with everyone. With a rich lady, for instance. He met her through his professor, and she thinks the world of him. She keeps inviting him to her huge apartment with its strange furniture and its maidservants. She sponsors and supports young artists and writers and, like many Munich natives, she feels "something like human sympathy with the revolution", as Graf says. She holds him in particularly high regard. At this time, Graf writes, it is the fashion for wealthy people to patronize a proletarian. And he has two of these patrons: one is the Dutchman, at whose house he is permitted to enjoy the good life as often as he wants, and the other is this rich lady, who gives him a monthly stipend of 200 marks. He passes the money on to Karoline, his unloved wife, and their baby, so she will leave him in peace. "I wrote poems and ran around with the revolutionaries," he writes.

But that isn't enough. It isn't enough. He has to express himself, he has to move people with his words. He wants to start a magazine, his own magazine. Intense writing, intense humanity. And money and power for its editor-in-chief: "I would sit at a desk smoking fat cigars, with a huge number of bells at hand; sub-editors, poets, reporters, lift-boys, and servants would run to carry out my instructions, I should be feared by the authorities and beloved by the people." Graf tells the Dutchman of his plan, and the Dutchman is instantly enthusiastic. He wants to take Graf to Frankfurt, introduce him to some important people, booksellers, funders, get Graf to explain his idea to them; it will be big, very big.

They travel to Frankfurt and alight at the Frankfurter Hof Hotel. Graf is intimidated by the glitz. "I had a luxurious room. I was literally intoxicated by such an overture to our adventure. I could already see myself as an all-powerful editor in a palatial newspaper office."

In the evening, the Dutchman introduces him to his rich friends. They have dinner in the hotel's grand dining room, and Graf quickly notices the waiters looking at him with condescension in their eyes. Then there are all the different glasses, all the plates, all the cutlery. He can't work it out. Oysters: how are you supposed to swallow them? The wealthy diners cast wry glances at him. The Dutchman gives a brief outline of the plan for the magazine, and his rich friend clears his throat: "Hmhm". Graf describes the kind of thing he wants to publish. Is anyone here interested? He starts to lose confidence. "And gradually everything slipped away. No one was interested. We drank and drank until well after closing time. At the end of the night we were all slumped in the darkened lobby of the hotel, everyone drunk, everyone lolling." The end of a magazine, of a dream. In drunkenness.

But Graf is not discouraged. Well then, he will speak to the people directly. He'll just shout his message of humanity straight into the ears of Munich's residents. Shake people awake. This might not be the time for writing, anyway. He will speak in front of as many people as possible, in the Mathäserbräu, the heroic cellar of that heroic November night. He tells the rich lady about his plan. She is delighted with it and gives him 2,000 marks to put it into action. Graf goes into a spin, prints posters: "People from every walk of life! Great Public Meeting! Against Terrorism! For Humanity! Speaker: Oskar Maria Graf, Munich", and at the end: "People! Gather! Say no! All you who have not forgotten your humanity, come!"

He plasters the whole city with them. "Have you written your speech?" the rich lady asks. "Oh yes," says Graf. His friends ask him, too: "Oskar? The speech?" Why all the concern, people? What needs to be said will become apparent once he takes the stage. The main thing is to get everyone there.

Everyone is there. The cellar is full to bursting, and outside people are packed into the garden as well. Graf has trouble forging a path to the podium. Tense expectation. He climbs up; to his right sits Mirjam Sachs, "the black girl", ready to transcribe the great speech he is about to give. "All you who are gathered here! People! Rebels! Citizens!" he shouts. Then he thinks for a moment. Nothing else occurs to him. People are fidgeting at the tables. He explains that he has brought them here to make a clear statement against terrorism. A heckler calls out from somewhere in the crowd. Now he is all at sea: he stutters, can't think what to say next. The audience is growing restive. The meeting's chairman rings the bell; Graf hopes he will ring it even louder. "Get him off!" someone yells. At the back a worker makes such loud threats that a fist fight breaks out. The communists on the right-hand side of the room start yelling. Graf shouts in their direction: "I'm against all terrorism! No matter where it comes from!" Now there is complete chaos. The Spartacist Joseph Sontheimer storms the podium, bellowing that Graf is a harmless Tolstoyan and very confused. Graf cries: "Enough! This meeting is over!" And he looks out into the seething crowd, the people gradually starting to disperse, calling out from all sides: "This toerag whips up half of Munich and then doesn't say anything! He wants a good beating!" The next day the papers are full of malice and mockery.

With the rest of the lady's money, Graf and a few of his friends found a "league of free people". They decide to build settlements in the countryside, where they mean to lead a free life and bring word of the glorious revolution to the rural population. The lady even provides yet more money for the enterprise. The friends move out, buy a run-down farm for an incredible sum from the snickering rural population, and come back to the city after just a few weeks, disillusioned. The wealthy lady isn't upset. She has done her bit for the revolution.

Very well then. For the time being, Graf decides to return to poetry. And he keeps visiting the Dutchman, to drink and carouse.

Meanwhile, the man who had sent a postcard welcoming Oskar Maria Graf's new magazine with such warm words is in no mood for carousing. And when Thomas Mann is invited to a small gathering and meets Rilke and various other famous people, who all seem to have played a part in the turbulent events of these days, he notes in his diary with a great deal of self-pity: "Realized that I live a solitary, withdrawn, brooding, peculiar, and sad existence."

In these winter weeks, he is preoccupied with money matters. He buys a "French marble relief and a small Dutch old master" for 34,000 marks, to secure his money and protect it from devaluation. He has to visit the dentist almost every day—as his readers know from the fate of Thomas Buddenbrook, dental health is an area in which he is particularly sensitive and anxious—and he is also having a bust made and has to sit for the sculptor on a regular basis.

But once, he finds time to attend a sitting of the Landtag with his mother-in-law. He is horrified: it's worse than he thought. But interesting, too. "The air dreadful. The behaviour of the meeting chaotic, childish and vulgar. The leadership incompetent. The result negative. But you see human types: nowhere are they presented more vividly than as speakers in discussions. I really must utilize the passion of the age and attend more meetings."

He won't make it to very many. The event in the National Theatre is another thing he only learns about from hearsay: "Stories of yesterday's 'Celebration of the Revolution' in the National Theatre, at which (with the exception of me, as I did not pay any attention to it), the entire literary and artistic world seems to have been present. The proceedings are said to have been dignified, but the mood largely sceptical. The royal boxes filled with the commonest crowd. Frau Auer, a bourgeois little wife and mother, as Minister of the Interior." He has also turned away from the Prime Minister again: "Tasteless Eisner, short Jewish man with a long beard, giving his address in front of the great curtain rather than speaking from a box. Someone told me Goethe would have turned in his grave."

And when Thomas Mann does attend an event that winter, his sights are suddenly set elsewhere: "I was absorbed in admiring an elegant young man with a gracefully foolish, boyish face, blond, refined, rather frail German type, somewhat reminiscent of Requadt. Seeing him unquestionably affected me in a way I have not noted in myself for a long time." And what now? "I readily admit to myself that this could turn into an experience." The next day: "I should like to try my luck and see the young man from yesterday again." The following morning he notes: "Frost. Slept uneasily as a result of the evening's erotic thoughts."

Once, at the start of December, he goes out walking with a handsome student. His name is Trummler and he tells Mann about the youth movement, about plans for a kind of "otherworldly commune of teachers with their students". Evidently a young follower of the German Wandervogel movement. Thomas Mann is very interested: "These young people are nothing less than rationalists. They yearn very much for mythical connections, they are national in their outlook (in my view, a thoroughly appropriate outlook), which means they detest the 'English' German, the imperialist and the global businessman. They want what is earthy and genuine—that, for them, is the reality of what it means to be human, not an abstract concept based on reason, then, not internationalism; a universalist humanity. Not bad at all."

A few weeks later he attends a lecture by Hans Blüher, the influential ideologue of the Wandervögel, whose descriptions of homoerotic male friendships, sometimes tinged with anti-Semitism, have proved very popular in the movement. Thomas Mann is delighted with what he hears. "An excellent lecture; almost every word of it spoke to my soul." Blüher, who is working on the second volume of his work *The Role of Eroticism in Male Society*, recommends to his audience one book in particular. It is by one of the political fighters of the day, whom Kurt Eisner called to Munich on the day he entered government, "to influence the minds of the people". The book is called *For Socialism*, and it was written by Gustav Landauer.

Thomas Mann buys it the very next day and, not long after, remarks: "I like much that Landauer's book has to offer. But in human practice things turn out differently."

Thomas Mann is still hoping for a German centre ground. "Really it is incumbent upon Germany to invent something new in politics, between Bolshevism and Western plutocracy." On the day of the election, he and his wife give their votes to the German People's Party.

Then comes the 21st of February. A warm, sunny spring day. Thomas Mann corrects the proofs of a newspaper article and does some work on *The Song of the Little Child*. His mother drops by briefly and is soon gone again. Then his wife bursts into his study with terrible news.

Kurt Eisner didn't want any guards. Nor did he want to take the route through the Bayerische Hof Hotel, the rear exit of which was directly opposite the Landtag building. This morning he wanted to walk upright, proud and dignified, accompanied only by his secretary Felix Fechenbach and colleague Benno Merkle, from his ministry to the Landtag, from one front door to the other, to announce his resignation and the resignation of his government.

Fechenbach had warned him—in fact, every colleague who had his best interests at heart had warned him. They had pointed to all the bile-filled threatening letters that he received on a daily basis, and to the press, which since his performance in Bern had been locked in mortal combat with him, making up stories and spreading rumours about his background. Notes like the one Eisner had read out at his last appearance in the theatre, about the governor whose time was up, were being distributed all over the city.

But Kurt Eisner had told a deeply worried Fechenbach: "You cannot avoid an assassination attempt for ever, and after all, I can only be shot dead once..."

One minute to ten. Eisner leaves the ministry. Fechenbach on his left, Merkle on his right, Kurt Eisner in the middle. He is carrying his resignation speech in his briefcase. They walk across Promenadenplatz. There are very few people about on this splendid morning; the streets that lead to the Landtag are closed off with military roadblocks. The three men turn onto Promenadenstraße. They have gone a few paces when they hear the crack of two gunshots in quick succession. Eisner sways for a moment; he tries to say something but he can't. Then he collapses without a sound. Kurt Eisner is dead.

One of the last poems he wrote in these days is entitled "Last March":

Pace by pace
Oh friend, we'll face
Dire need;
It lends us speed.
Look and see
How time flees
Through a flood
Of human blood.
We never cease
Pursuing peace
The city wakes:
A sombre horde
Now walks abroad
Stalked by traitors
Pace by pace,
Death shows his face.

Lift up your chin:
Since we began, you were a man!
Have faith
and win!

Kurt Eisner has barely hit the ground when more shots are fired. Benno Merkle looks round. He sees the Prime Minister's body prostrated on the pavement, a lake of blood already forming around his head. Where did the shots come from? He catches sight of a man in a gateway, and then three soldiers with rifles at the ready rush towards Merkle, calling out: "Into the Landtag! Let's clean up in there!"

Merkle brings the soldiers over to Eisner's body: "Look! This is the man you want to avenge. If he were able to speak a few final words now, he would say: do not avenge me." Merkle's words and the look on the silent Eisner's face make such an impression on the soldiers that they return to their posts.

But more and more people rush over. Eisner's body is taken into the porter's lodge at the ministry and laid on a sofa. The man in the gateway who, when the second volley rang out, also collapsed as if dead, has been dragged inside a house and the door locked behind him. It is Count Arco. He was waiting for the Prime Minister in the entrance to an apartment building on the public side of the roadblock, and shot him twice in the back of the head.

He too was badly wounded by several bullets. At once, an angry mob surrounded the man on the floor with the intention of carrying him off. But on Merkle's instructions he was taken to safety. Count Arco had assumed that he too would die in the attack and had therefore written a note outlining his motive in advance: "My reason: I hate Bolshevism, I love my Bavarian people, I am a faithful royalist, a good Catholic.

And above all I respect the honour of Bavaria. Eisner is a Bolshevist. He is a Jew. He is no German. He is betraying the Fatherland—and so..."

All the ministers and MPs are gathered in the Landtag. Every last seat on the benches is occupied. The Workers' Council has taken all the tickets for itself. At nine o'clock there had been a meeting of the party leaders, and Auer, with a beam of triumphal joy on his face, had informed the gathering that the previous night he had succeeded in persuading Eisner to abdicate. In his ten o'clock speech, he would be announcing his resignation.

So now everyone is waiting for the speech. It is ten past ten, and upstairs in the diplomats' box the door opens and a blood-spattered sailor approaches the SPD's Ernst Niekisch, head of the Central Council, and Frau Eisner, who is sitting beside him. He taps her with his forefinger and pants: "Eisner has been shot."

The regional leader of the conservative German Democratic Party, Ernst Müller-Meiningen, says of these seconds: "A tremendous excitement came over the assembly, particularly on the overcrowded benches. Everyone had the feeling that unusual things, things never before seen in the history of the parliament, would now occur. Fechenbach, Eisner's adjutant, pale and still wearing his hat, pushed his way through the crowd of MPs and shouted something to Auer, who was sitting in the second minister's seat on the left side of the chamber." Evidently he blames Auer for his adversary's murder. Minister Frauendorfer cries: "Insolent boy!"

The excitement grows from one minute to the next. Before long the Father of the House, Dr Jäger, opens the meeting: "Ladies and gentlemen! Before we begin this session, I must make it known that there is a rumour Prime Minister Eisner has been shot and killed today. The murderer is said to have been shot dead as well. The matter is of course extremely distressing for us in both human and political terms." He welcomes the assembled crowd, nominates two secretaries, and says that at the request of the honourable member Dr Süßheim, the session will be adjourned for an hour.

The news quickly spreads through the city. In some churches, the bells start to toll. Is it just a rumour? Is it the truth? Hasn't everyone been expecting this exact news for weeks?

Alois Lindner is a powerfully built man with a moustache, a flat cap and large, bulging eyes. He works as a barman in the central station. He was born in Kelheim, Lower Bavaria, was apprenticed to a butcher in Regensburg and then drifted through Germany and Switzerland. In Hamburg he took a job on an ocean liner and travelled the world. He disembarked in New York and worked as a cowboy in Texas, living there for a few months with a Native American woman. Then he went back to sea, spent a year working in a canning factory in Australia, and learnt of the outbreak of the world war while on the Suez Canal. After various adventures he reached Munich, where not long after his arrival he heard Kurt Eisner speak out against the war for the first time and joined him enthusiastically. He didn't miss a single one of his speeches, a single public meeting.

The revolution, the 7th of November and the days that followed were the happiest days of his life. He was a devotee, a believer. Later he recalled: "Kurt Eisner, released from prison, lifted up our hearts. He called us to defend the revolution, to defend socialism. We were firmly resolved. 'Forward, victory is ours!' So it went on for days and nights. Eventually I could do no more. I collapsed from tiredness and exhaustion. When

I awoke, I thought it had all been a dream. I had experienced the revolution not with my head but with my heart. And from then on my heart beat faster, embracing all those brothers and sisters who like me were reaching for the stars. We had tested and measured our strength, we became one through our actions. Before us, beloved and honoured, stood our leader, Kurt Eisner."

Alois Lindner was one of the group of workers who had gone to Erhard Auer's apartment in December and forced him to resign. He hated Eisner's opponent with the same burning zeal that he brought to his love for the Prime Minister.

And now the Prime Minister was dead. By this point the bells were ringing for all they were worth. "We were destroyed," Lindner writes later. "These bullets had not struck a man; they had struck freedom, the revolution." The cry echoed around the city streets: "Revenge for Eisner!" Again and again, louder and louder: "Revenge for Eisner!" Followed by the battle cry: "Down with the traitor Auer!"

Lindner races towards parliament. He is clutching a Browning. No one stops him. He enters the debating chamber just after eleven. And whom does he see at the lectern? Who is giving a speech about his dead hero? It cannot be. Erhard Auer is there at the lectern, referring to Eisner as the "provisional Prime Minister", crying out: "We mourn the murdered man as the leader of the revolution in Bavaria, and also as a man filled with the purest idealism and a loyal concern for the proletariat."

Alois Lindner later wrote: "The tears of rage, flowing inwards, lit flames in my soul. I raised my arm. The flash from the pistol ripped the veil from my eyes. My temples throbbed quietly. No more shouting and screaming for revenge! I have avenged the dead man!"

Ernst Müller-Meiningen saw "a man in an overcoat, like a chauffer's coat, taking great, ominous strides towards the Social Democrat benches, making a swift turn to the right as if in an exercise yard, and now taking two large paces straight towards Minister Auer... He raised a Browning, calmly took aim at the far end of the ministers' row and fired two shots at Auer, who was just about to get up, with the cry 'blackguard'... He fired several more times at the other ministers, who after the first volley had ducked under their bench."

Chaos, more shooting, fear. Running, shouting, fleeing. Auer has fallen off his seat. An unknown person in the gallery fires down at the scattering members of parliament like a real marksman. It looks like there might be a massacre. Heinrich Osel, an MP from the Bavarian People's Party, is hit and collapses. Alois Lindner heads for the exit; a major tries to stop him, there is a tussle, a gunshot, and the major sinks to the floor. Lindner climbs the stairs to the gallery. An MP tells the soldiers to arrest him. Ernst Müller-Meiningen hears Alois Lindner shouting to the soldiers: "You're with us! You're not going to touch me!" After which the soldiers explain that "the whole business was nothing to do with them. Auer had got his just deserts."

Heinrich Osel is dead. Major Paul Ritter von Jahreiß is dead. Auer is alive, but badly wounded. The Finance Minister, Edgar Jaffé, keeps calling for a doctor. The members run down the corridors in a blind panic. Soldiers with bayonets affixed approach them, shouting: "No one's getting out of the Landtag alive today. You'll all be killed!"

Some MPs have taken refuge in the party meeting rooms. Soldiers stand at the doors, to place anyone who comes out under immediate arrest. Many escape through the windows

and climb down the drainpipes. Outside, the Landtag guards
have turned their machine guns towards the building. Ernst
Niekisch asks the soldiers of the guard what on earth they
are doing, and they tell him they intend to gun down every
last member of parliament. They will all pay for Eisner's
death. Niekisch tries to persuade them that this is madness.
Muttering, they eventually turn the machine guns back round.
Without firing a shot.

Some of the soldiers form an escort for Alois Lindner, and
he stays with a comrade for a few days. After that, he will
shave off his beard and flee over the border to Austria, and
from there to Hungary.

Munich quakes. Hundreds gather around the large blood-
stain on Promenadenstraße. Soldiers have erected a pyramid
of rifles. People press handkerchiefs into the dried blood
on the ground, for a relic, and clutch it to their breasts.
Then sawdust is scattered over the blood. Women weep,
soon some men are weeping too. "Our Eisner! Our one and
only Eisner!" a woman sobs. On Promenadenplatz a truck
full of soldiers with red flags and machine guns drives past
and shouts are heard: "Revenge for Eisner!" People distribute
new flyers, calling for a general strike and railing against
"slanderous agitation by a venal press". "Down with the bourgeoisie and their criminal accomplices! Long live the socialist
revolution!"

Oskar Maria Graf writes: "One read it almost greedily.
I saw people trembling, pale with rage and hungry for blood.
Everywhere, the same calls for revenge. The crowds began to
surge, they flowed through the city. It was different, entirely
different from the 7th of November. If someone had stood
up now and cried out: 'Slaughter the bourgeoisie! Set fire to
the city! Destroy everything!' it would have happened. A

thousand little storms had come together, and a single, dull, dark, uncertain eruption began. I could feel it most acutely in myself: never had I been so fully part of the masses as now. The crowds headed for the Theresienwiese. Many people spoke under the statue of Bavaria; Toller read a poem. The women were captivated by it, the men shouted for weapons."

Ernst Toller had been in Bern with Eisner, had seen him captivate and thrill the international socialists. But rather than travel back with Eisner he had spent a few days in St Moritz, where the *jeunesse dorée* of all countries had gathered. "In fashionable garments, dripping with diamonds and pearls, they play-acted international peace like the phantoms and *lemures* of a forgotten world," he wrote of them.

On 21st February, Toller returned. From his compartment he heard the excited shouts of a Swiss train conductor, and inside, the hearty "Bravo" of a bourgeois German. He didn't understand the words that reached his ears, but eventually he caught their meaning: Kurt Eisner had been murdered. Toller knew, of course, what danger Eisner had been in. He also knew it had been Eisner's disregard for his own safety that had set him apart from all the republican ministers. People had felt his fearlessness in the face of death and believed in him because of it. His whole life was dedicated to his convictions. "There are always plenty of talented men," Toller wrote later, "but the masses will only follow those who have obviously overcome the fear of death."

Will they soon be following *him*?

Cheering breaks out in Klaus Mann's school. Among the teachers, among the students. The young Klaus notes in his diary that on hearing the news, he himself burst into tears. But later he writes that this was not quite the truth. He had mostly been glad that, following the announcement, all the students had been sent home and given the rest of the day off. In his Eisner play, which he will write that same year, young Klaus gives his hero Eisner an almost Shakespearian monologue: "But how beautiful I thought it to liberate a people, to deliver, to govern, to be a father to them! Those are lost illusions. I am challenged from all sides. Nothing is so hard as man's ingratitude! I stand on quaking feet. Wilhelm Herzog has left for Berlin.—I, however, stand my ground. Even if the people should kill me, I will remain their father."

Planes circle over the city, dropping flyers. The population is instructed to keep the peace and not to go out after seven o'clock. The trams have stopped running. It lends the inner city an unusual silence.

Josef Hofmiller, the German nationalist schoolteacher who is friends with the composer Hans Pfitzner and has recently published a glowing review of Mann's *Reflections of a Nonpolitical Man* in the *Süddeutsche Monatsheft*, had been teaching that morning. In the free periods that followed he was intending to pop out and buy a pound of semolina, but then the news of Eisner's murder reached him, too. Over the preceding weeks and months he had filled his diary with loathing and horror at the government; in his last entry he had written: "The thugocracy under which we live is becoming tedious." Even horror grows stale over time. It was only the Jews he was always able to get worked up about.

And now the top Jew is finally dead. Hofmiller sees "numerous people with conspicuously pleased expressions", who confirm the news to him. He also has the rest of the day off now, and he takes a stroll over to the scene of the crime. Sees the blood, sees an easel holding a picture of Kurt Eisner that someone has set up, sees the flowers and, in the faces of the people gathered there, "a certain satisfaction". In any case, the grief "did not seem too great".

In Hofmiller's opinion, the person with the greatest responsibility for Eisner's murder is the murdered man himself. "Everything Eisner did invoked a violent end," he writes. Now he thinks it unfortunate that the Prime Minister wasn't removed sooner. And they wouldn't necessarily have had to kill him, writes Hofmiller. When Eisner came back from Switzerland, they should have stopped his train between stations. "A platelayer with a red flag on the stretch of track outside Günzach, where the gradient is steepest and the locomotive can only proceed slowly, given the present shortage of coal: wave the flag, stop the train, and have half a dozen determined people quickly remove Eisner from the compartment and take him somewhere safe in this out-of-the-way spot." Josef Hofmiller has thought of everything. "They could, for example, have brought him to some isolated hunting cabin in the Ammergau Alps between Füssen and Murnau, demand that he resign and then get him over the border, take away his papers etc." In this way "we could have got rid of the troublemaker without any bloodshed". But no one asked Josef Hofmiller, and "so his violent death will spark a civil war".

The MPs have fled home, the government has disintegrated. Workers, sailors and soldiers waving red flags hasten to the National Theatre. The doors are locked, they kick them in, there are crashes, the tinkle of broken glass, everyone piles into the auditorium. A sailor roars: "The Workers' and Soldiers' Councils will meet here permanently from this day forth!" There is a wild hubbub of talking and shouting.

The councils gradually come together, people packed in tightly. "I could see nothing but backs, necks and hair, caps and hats," writes Oskar Maria Graf.

He can't believe that once again all people are doing is talking. The councils are meeting permanently? What good will that do? What is all the talk for? The city is quaking *now*! The revolution is at hand *now*!

"Get the newspapers!" he cries on his way out, to the people still trying to squeeze in. One of his comrades barges out with him. They run down Bayerstraße and see distant columns of smoke rising from the offices of the *Münchener Zeitung*. "The plague house is burning at last!" shouts a worker at his side. But the only thing burning is that day's edition of the paper, which the occupiers have hauled out onto the street and set alight. People are dancing around the flames. The Republican Guard is stationed outside the entrance.

The editorial offices of the *München-Augsburger Abend-zeitung* in Paul-Heyse-Straße are also occupied. Graf goes there, too. It's the paper that used to print his book reviews, until they stopped printing them. The old editors are still there. Suddenly so friendly towards Graf as he strides in: "Ah, Herr Graf, are you looking for the Workers' Council?" one of the editors asks him. "'No, no,' I smiled spitefully, 'I'm just happy that everything belongs to us now.'"

When he arrives home late that evening, his lodger greets him with revolutionary speeches. He hobbles around the room, excitedly telling Graf about hostages being taken, students cheering, and the university, that "terrible place", thankfully being closed down. He says that someone needs to arm the proletariat, straight away. And he adds casually: "They should hurry up and bring in the guillotines, as well."

Graf looks at him and gives a bitter laugh. He thinks, the whole German Revolution is just like this man: it has a club foot and limps. Graf laughs and says: "You're a symbol, man! A real symbol!"

But the lodger goes on talking like a mass murderer holding the reins of power. Graf starts to get annoyed. "Show me your hands, man!" he cries, and takes hold of the lodger's short, fleshy fingers: "You've never held a shovel, and you've never set foot in a factory!... Did the workers come calling for you?... Can't they do it without you?... It's people like you who'll get the guillotine!"

The lodger looks shocked, calls Graf a counter-revolutionary: "If you weren't a great poet, I'd denounce you on the spot... Be careful I don't put you up against the wall."

Graf retorts: "Oh of course, that's the easiest work there is, denouncing people and putting them up against the wall." He goes out into the night. There is a curfew. The streets are completely silent. How can I be useful to the revolution? he wonders. Who needs me now? He thinks of the Dutchman, who has moved to a new villa in Nymphenburg. He walks out of the city, and the darkness intensifies. He can't even see any lighted windows now. "The cold wind swept round the corners and hurled itself at me. I felt an uneasy sense of rootlessness."

The villa is magnificent. The painter Heinrich Maria Davringhausen has also been drawn into the Dutchman's drinking and carousing circle, and Marietta is there. They drink schnapps, dine at a richly decked table, lounge in comfortably upholstered armchairs, smoke cigars. A servant brings out sparkling wine, corks pop. "Now, perhaps, we have reached a point where people's wealth will be confiscated," Oskar Maria Graf remarks as if in passing.

———

The city is quieter than it has ever been. "The silence has the air of that strange silence before an earthquake, when one hears the frightened birds chirping," writes the poet Ricarda Huch, in her flat at the rear of a building on Kaulbachstraße, where she lives with her eighteen-year-old daughter. "We began to suspect that the bullet that hit Eisner had ushered in a new epoch of the revolution."

Huch's poems sell by the hundreds of thousands; she has also written a vast work on Romanticism and one on the Thirty Years' War, which was admired by both Rilke and Thomas Mann. She stood in the January election as a candidate for the German Democratic Party, but wasn't voted in. For a while she was part of the Council of Intellectual Workers, but instantly quarrelled with its pacifist members and left after three weeks. She is a natural conservative, but in these days she responds to a questionnaire in the Social Democrat paper *Vorwärts* by saying: "Socialism must provide a counterbalance to an exaggerated individualism. This is the path on which our future lies. Choosing to come together now will one day allow people to lead strong, individual lives."

She, too, is filled with horror at Eisner's murder: "Everyone damned and deplored young Arco's fateful bullets. It was as if they were fired purely to give fresh impetus to the faltering revolution." But from the very beginning she has thought his rule was a misunderstanding, a misunderstanding between him and the Bavarian people: "They understood Eisner as little as he understood them. And how should they? There was not a single drop or a crumb of royal Bavarian conviviality, crudeness, slovenliness and bonhomie in him; he was an abstract moralist, who apparently wrote some very good theatre reviews and certainly wrote some bad poems. But criticism and theory make neither a good ruler nor a good artist; one has to be able to *do* it."

When she hears that people have been dipping their handkerchiefs in the dead man's blood, she bursts out laughing and tells her daughter Marietta: "In short, madness has triumphed!"

But there is something she finds more despicable still, a new development that she has not previously observed to this extent, but which seems to characterize the age in which she lives. Ricarda Huch writes: "A particularly obnoxious feature of our time and a clear sign of our civilization's degeneration, it seems to me, is that nothing can happen without it at once being photographed and cinematographed. It is the most extreme level of self-display: mankind lives in front of the mirror. Perhaps eventually even murderers and burglars will not be able to resist having their crimes cinematographed, and so eventually crime will die out through the sheer awareness of it."

On the very day of his murder, people all over the city started selling portraits of Eisner and postcards of the crime scene. In the days and weeks that followed, the images were everywhere. Through his death, Kurt Eisner had become a symbol of the Bavarian Revolution. Portraits of him became the saints' cards of that epoch. His death had changed everything. Ricarda Huch heard a girl on the street saying: "It's funny, but almost every day I used to hear someone sigh: is there no bullet yet with Eisner's name on it? And since he was shot, everyone has been lamenting his death and cursing his murderer."

In the Huch household at least, there is laughter on this silent evening until late into the night. A friend came to visit just before the start of the curfew, and now she can't leave and they laugh together—"perhaps all the more boisterously because a dark awareness of danger and horror was lurking in the corners of our minds".

On the other side of the Isar, on the Herzogpark, there also lurks an awareness of danger on this late evening. It's less silent here than in the city centre. There is an intermittent crackle of gunfire. Or is Thomas Mann imagining it? Are those shots just the sound of the fear inside him? He and his wife have spent the whole day on the telephone, having taken the children for a walk along the Isar in the morning. Klaus of course gave a lively account of how his fellow students cheered and danced when the news of Eisner's murder reached them. "The sheer senselessness of Arco's deed had to be immediately evident at this moment," Thomas Mann wrote in his diary. And after hearing about the occupation of all the newspaper offices: "We have a soviet government á la russe." Then the telephone again. Most often, it's Bruno Walter's wife. She reports that people are hunting for aristocrats in the city and in their neighbourhood. The hunters have already been to Baron Rummel's house. He served them wine. A day of comedy and fear, panic and comedy.

That evening at a quarter past ten there is a sudden bang very close to the Mann villa. Clearly hand grenades, thinks the man of the house, suspecting that a front door, not opened voluntarily, has been blown off. Afterwards he hears wild shouting. He goes out onto the balcony with Katia in the dark. He writes: "Quiet followed. Agitated. I do not think they will be coming to us."

Meanwhile, shortly after midnight, the man who imposed the curfew is on his way from the office back to his hotel when he is stopped by a military patrol who ask to see his pass. That day he has signed something like 400 passes for council members who are permitted to be out in the city at night—but he hasn't signed one for himself. He is the Social Democrat Ernst Niekisch, who on this day when the Bavarian government evaporated has somehow found himself in charge. As leader of the Central Council, the sudden power vacuum has given him control of the government. The new head of state now finally wants to get back to his hotel—but the military patrol doesn't know him. They've never heard of him. And whoever he is, he doesn't have a pass. They take him to the police station. The Chief of Police is still there; he is called in, recognizes Niekisch at once, and the two of them laugh and laugh and the patrol escorts Bavaria's new leader back to his hotel.

The next day, Kurt Eisner's body is laid out at the eastern cemetery, the Ostfriedhof in Giesing. He lies on a white, lace-trimmed sheet in a white burial gown. A bunch of tulips has been placed in the open coffin, and his white hands are folded in his lap. Beard and hair combed, the high white forehead, the coffin surrounded by asters and hyacinths and fir branches. A peaceful image.

The funeral takes place five days later, on 26th February. A hundred thousand people join the funeral procession. They meet on the Theresienwiese, where the adventure began three months and nineteen days earlier. They have been asked not to wear top hats. Unionists and corporations are told to gather around the bands and choirs in a horseshoe formation. The mourners who don't belong to a particular organization are asked to stand to the right and follow the instructions of the marshals. This information is displayed on posters all over the city. They also say that the choirs will sing the funeral march from Wagner's *Twilight of the Gods*, and Beethoven's "The Heavens are Telling".

An endless black procession slowly starts to move. It looks as though the whole of Munich is dressed in black. Bells toll all over the city. The cortege is headed by a band from the former Royal Infantry Lifeguards Regiment and the choir of the National Theatre. Then come artists, representatives of the city of Munich and "well-known figures from the Social Democratic parties" such as Ernst Niekisch. Then people bearing wreaths, delegations from all the Munich regiments, Russian prisoners of war, the Bavarian colliers. A portrait of the dead man is held aloft. Many of the houses are flying red and black flags. Twenty bands are distributed at intervals among the mourners. The front of the procession halts at the statue of Bavaria, and the choirs strike up Kurt Eisner's "Song of the People", written in the days of his rule, to the melody of the victory hymn "We Gather Together". And Munich sings:

> We call as we fall
> On the stars far above us;
> They blink as they sink
> And plunge into the night.
> The masses throw off
> Their misgivings, start living,
> For freedom is calling
> In a halo of light.
>
> Our age is enraged
> And the earth quakes in anger
> The claws of the old
> Clutch the heart of the new.
> The pale and the stale
> Will be left now to languor,
> The people have woken
> And bid death adieu.

We gather together,
Hear liberty calling,
We defend to the end
This, our sacred decree.
We gather together
In common endeavour
A new Reich is born:
Oh world, thou art free!
Oh world, thou art free!

The socialist fairy-tale king's song to the future. His hymn. The hymn of his revolution.

At the Ostfriedhof, the crowd starts backing up. Only a small circle of relatives and socialist politicians are admitted to the funeral service in the cemetery hall. The political stars of the day pull up in grand horse-drawn carriages. Gustav Landauer, whom Eisner had called to his side on the first day of his rule to exert his influence on the nation's soul, climbs out of his carriage wearing a long black overcoat, with the dignity of a new king. He will give the central speech; the communist Levien and the ministers Unterleitner and Jaffé will speak, too. An address by Heinrich Mann has also been announced.

As the funeral service begins in the Ostfriedhof, the end of the procession has not yet even set off from the Theresienwiese. Everyone wants to be there when the first king of this new, turbulent age is laid to rest.

Landauer starts to speak: "This man of the intellect, who required solitude for himself and his inner life, yearned for a beautiful connection with his brothers in man for the sake of his soul's peace." He recalls the verse written by the eighteen-year-old Eisner: "The one true life is lived in others, and when we die, we walk alone." He celebrates the "dead man who shines in transfigured sovereignty", and says that Eisner's "prickly severity" had been as necessary as "the whip with which Jesus Christ chased the money-changers from the temple". He speaks of Eisner's "childlike quality" and his "longing to be permitted a childlike happiness".

And he goes on: "Kurt Eisner, the Jew, was a prophet who wrestled mercilessly with faint-hearted, pitiful men, because he loved mankind and believed in it and wanted it. He was a prophet because he empathized with the poor and the downtrodden and saw the possibility, the necessity, of bringing poverty and subjugation to an end. He was a prophet because he saw and *understood*—this poet, who both dreamt of the beauty he wanted to see in the world and looked the hard, evil facts in the eye, undaunted."

And he closes with a mission. For everyone: "The revolution is his bequest to mankind. We must go on with it, steadfastly and humanely."

Silence. Then a group of sailors carries Eisner's coffin away for cremation.

Heinrich Mann is somewhat surprised. Doesn't he get a turn? What about his speech? He has prepared the whole thing. He was going to say: "The hundred days of Eisner's government brought forth more ideas, more joys of reason, more enlivenment of the spirits than the preceding fifty years." He was going to cry out to the mourners: "His belief in the power of thought to transform itself into reality captivated even the unbelievers. Spirit is truth!" He was going to take the derisory term that his brother had invented for him in *Reflections of a Nonpolitical Man* and use it with pride to describe the dead man, posthumously declaring him his brother and comrade in the fight for freedom. "Any man who is so steadfast in his passion for the truth, and for that very reason so mild when it comes to humanity, deserves the honour of being called a 'literatus of civilization'. Kurt Eisner was such a man."

It is not until three weeks later, at another memorial service in the Odeon, that Heinrich Mann will be able finally to deliver his speech. His brother will hear about it from his friend Ernst Bertram. Especially that passage. He will note Heinrich saying "that Eisner had deserved the honour of being called a 'literatus of civilization'. *Not* nauseating..."

Now, on this black 26th of February in the year 1919, the large black crowd takes a long time to disperse. People press forward towards the cremation hall. They are still hoping to glimpse the coffin of their fairy-tale king, who had to die before becoming their hero, the city's hero, the hero of the revolution. And there in the crowd is a thin, pale man with an unusual moustache. Isn't that him—the man who will later claim he wasn't even in the city at the time? The drifting, unsuccessful painter, friendless but for the trade unionist Ernst Schmidt and his comrades in the regiment. Years later, while serving a prison sentence in a fortress, he will write: "I, however, now resolved to become a politician"—and date that decision as November 1918, the month of the German defeat and the German Revolution. But Adolf Hitler hasn't made any decisions yet. He still has no idea what purpose life has in store for him. He is still—probably—a small part of this vast, mourning crowd, accompanying the peculiar people's king of Bavaria on his final journey.

Early in his existence, the people's king himself had imagined his end in much more prosaic terms than those of the poetic eulogists at his funeral. In 1888, at the age of twenty-one, he had written a little verse "for my biographer, i.e. gravestone poet":

Here lies Kurt Eisner
And the plans in his head.
We doubted his genius;
We're sure that he's dead.

A MUNICH OF POSSIBILITIES

IN THE DAYS that followed Eisner's death, Munich's reputation reverberated throughout Europe. What had been accomplished here, after the war, was simply incredible. The fact that a long-haired theatre critic had seized an opportune moment one night and put himself in the prime minister's seat—and had simply stayed there and ruled—was fantastic! A writer! A dreamer! A mystical revolutionary! And in Germany of all places, a swaggering country bristling with weapons, a country its neighbours had learnt to fear in recent years. That could not, that *must* not be undone by a lone fanatic's gunshot. And everyone could see that the city was still standing behind its Prince Charming, even in death, as 100,000 people laid him to rest with such pomp and dignity. "Oh world, thou art free!" had been his parting words, his message to everyone. And many, many people now came to rejoice in their freedom, here in the capital of this happy movement.

There was no government now. Or rather: there were two governments, and both were getting on with the business of governing without greatly disturbing the populace. The Central Council continued to exist; it now claimed absolute authority and reconvened the Congress of Councils. Meanwhile, the elected parliamentarians who hadn't fled the city immediately after Eisner's murder held meetings in private apartments to vote on how to proceed, and to elect a new government. On a visit to the crime scene a few days after the murder they met with the Chief of Police, and some MPs announced they would resume party meetings in the Landtag the following day. But the Chief of Police told them he couldn't guarantee their safety. And the soldiers of the Republican Guard stationed outside the Landtag made it abundantly clear to the parliamentarians that, in the event of an attack, they should under no circumstances count on the Guard's assistance. And so the MPs left the city and resumed their meetings at the start of March, alternating between Nuremberg and Bamberg, to negotiate the formation of a new government. The head of the German Democratic Party in Bavaria, Ernst Müller-Meiningen, described the mobile negotiations outside Munich: "On Sunday, late in the evening, we got in a large truck—Social Democrats, Democrats, Bavarian People's Party, all quite amicable—and drove from Nuremberg to Bamberg, where we discussed how the government should be formed and drafted a programme for government until long after midnight."

Putting together another cabinet will be more difficult. Fearing the power of the streets, the Social Democrats are adamant that the USPD should have a cabinet position again despite their devastating election defeat. Very well, writes Müller-Meiningen, then let us reappoint Hans Unterleitner as Minister for Social Welfare: "The parties considered Unterleitner, the blunt instrument of Eisner's ministry, to be less dangerous in than out." Eventually they have a full complement of ministers. But the most difficult problem is: under these circumstances, out here, who wants to be prime minister of a government in exile?

The Congress of Councils in Munich has installed the SPD's Martin Segitz as their leader, which makes him unelectable for the MPs in their mobile parliament. "We saw Johannes Hoffmann, who had until that point been Culture Minister, as the only serious contender. He caused great difficulties." Hoffmann had been a schoolteacher, but was dismissed in 1908 for his undisguised sympathies with the SPD. In his short time as a minister in Eisner's government, he had instituted an anti-clerical education policy that had made the Catholic Church's blood boil. "Piquant" is what Müller-Meiningen calls the situation. "This man, of all people, whom the Bavarian People's Party had cursed as a devil incarnate, a godless man... was now being begged by that same party to stand 'as the only suitable candidate'." With the threat of death hanging over him, and with no real power, no official residence, no capital city—no, Johannes Hoffmann didn't exactly push himself forward for this post.

But the Munich Central Council doesn't feel it has full power during these weeks, either. The SPD's Ernst Niekisch presides over the Central Council. He complains: "It is truly unpleasant to be the responsible government and to be patronized and treated like nincompoops. Even I am sometimes filled with rage."

It is more pleasant not to govern. It is more pleasant to make use of the freedoms of this ungoverned city, in this ungoverned state. These weeks see the arrival of dreamers, winter-sandal-wearers, preachers, plant-whisperers, the liberated and the liberators, long-haired men, hypnotists and those who have been hypnotized, drifters. Anyone coming to this luminous city is themselves illuminated. Gustav Regler later recalls: "I arrived in Munich with scanty luggage and little money, confused but with the feeling of having reached a new and better land."

A few years earlier the Berlin author and dramatist Friedrich Freska had written a novel called *Phosphorus*, about a stuffy bourgeois man who, following a blow to the head, becomes an easy-going bon viveur and ladykiller. Now Freska saw his novel transformed into reality as he arrived in Bavaria's capital city. "But what was going on here? Was this still Munich? No, it was a southern city! Ragged people were sunning themselves on the steps. Women sat out on the porticos of the buildings with their children. There were bright red, green and blue blankets; the Lazzaroni had moved in."

The war hero Wilhelm Schramm, who due to his extraordinary military accomplishments had been allowed to call himself by the noble title Wilhelm Ritter von Schramm, was deeply shaken by the transformation of his city into a carnival town of prophets and saviours: "Radical elements from all over the world had gathered here, deserters and many so-called artists, international men of letters and Jewish intellectuals, who often didn't even speak German—there was no doubt that now the thousand-year kingdom of earthly happiness had to begin. On every street corner, prophets great and small spoke—nay, preached—about this humanity and its kingdom, which would encompass all nations or rather the proletariats of all nations, and every day crowds formed around them. One of these prophets called himself Neander and was not afraid to call on God and Christ Himself to return as the chief witnesses and divine patrons of the socialist revolution."

When he wasn't drinking with the Dutchman, Oskar Maria Graf walked the streets of this drunken city, entirely baffled by it: "At that time a huge number of odd characters appeared. One of them wore a long pigtail and a straw hat, tight checked trousers, and a heavy jacket of the same cloth. He sought out crowds and whispered in everyone's ear: 'We are the Christ! Be calm, children of men! Do not make your own cross!' And he vanished as quickly as he had arrived. Another—a ragged man with a pinched, ill-humoured face—spent most of his time sitting in the cafés, doing sums. He drew up charts on long sheets of white paper, and if anyone spoke to him he would declare with a snort that if each person ate no more than ninety grams of rye bread and ten of meat a day, there would be an end to penury. He was especially enraged by patisserie. If he found himself in front of a display of cakes, he would instantly start ranting: 'Well, well, Herr Neighbour, well! Just look at this!... This luxury will be our ruin... The pastry chef is the greatest criminal of all... action must be taken against him...'"

Graf looked, listened, noted and marvelled: "Christians preached in meetings, proponents of nudism broadcast their beliefs, individualists and Bible scholars, people announcing the coming of the thousand-year Reich, old codgers speaking in favour of polygamy, peculiar Darwinists and racial theorists, theosophers and spiritualists made a harmless nuisance of themselves. Once at night I was walking across the Stachus when a thin man darted towards me, pressed a slip of paper into my hands and hastily ran on into the murky darkness. I stopped under a street lamp and looked at the note. All it said was: 'The Jew is meddling in our affairs! Germans, bethink yourselves!'"

While all this was going on, the various governments were busily occupied with resolutions, socialization, legislation and self-affirmation. As early as 28th February, the anarchist Erich Mühsam, who never missed a demonstration, meeting, debate, talk or literary reading in these months, attended the Congress of Councils and requested that Bavaria proclaim itself a socialist council republic; the delegates rejected his request by 234 votes to 70. After that, the communists Max Levien and August Hagemeister left the Central Council, and the Communist Party headquarters in Berlin sent Eugen Leviné to Munich. He was a poet and a professional revolutionary, born in St Petersburg, educated in a Wiesbaden boarding school, and had been involved in all the focal points of the revolution since 1905. It was clear that the vacuum, the anarchy, would not last for ever.

And councils—that was the magic word in these days, the magic formula of hope for a better, communally organized world, to be negotiated anew every day. And not just as a supplement to a parliamentary democracy, either. No: councils as the sole system of government. The Council Republic. Looking back, Gustav Regler wrote: "They had a mysterious faith in the [...] councils or soviets—since to them these implied direct action, daily consultation with the masses, the approach to the roots of the community: a hazy conception of the ideals which drew the apostles to Jesus, and an uncritical enthusiasm for the Russian experiment."

An enthusiasm for the new age even runs through the villa on the Herzogpark. One day at a time, at least, on a trial basis. At first in the diary: "Insofar as the 'councils' keep the Mühsams of this world at bay," writes Thomas Mann, "I too am essentially in favour of them. I cannot want simple parliamentarianism. It comes down to 'inventing something new in politics', and more specifically something German." And when the rumour arises, seemingly requiring no basis whatsoever in fact, that the author of *Reflections of a Nonpolitical Man* has joined the Independent Social Democrats, he feels almost flattered: "I have a growing sympathy for what is healthy, human, national, anti-Entente, *anti-political* within Spartacism, Communism, Bolshevism. The rumour of my 'joining the USPD' is not meaningless."

After Béla Kun has declared Hungary a Republic of Councils on 21st March, Thomas Mann finally enters into the carnival mood. "Revolt against these bourgeois windbags!" "National uprising!" he drums out in his diary. He is ready for anything. "I can see myself going out into the street and shouting: 'Down with lying Western democracy! Hurrah for Germany and Russia! Hurrah for communism!'"

Events in Hungary have led to a new mood all over the city. There can be no more freewheeling through this political landscape. The question of real power is becoming ever more pressing. It is still there for the taking. When are people going to get serious about their own Bavarian Council Republic, if not now? But the left-wing factions are keeping a close eye on each other. There is no trust between the Social Democrats, the Independent Social Democrats, the anarchists and the communists. Who will take the first step? Who will take up the reins of leadership? Who has the courage to fail?

Perhaps it will be the polemicist who was so excited to have Thomas Mann look at his poems; he became the head of the USPD in Munich on 9th March, and ever since has suffered angry assaults from the communists, mocking his pleas for a non-violent revolution. Ernst Toller.

"How do you make an omelette without breaking eggs?" was the headline of a vicious attack by the communist Max Levien in the *Rote Fahne* on 25th March. The dictatorship of the proletariat could only be achieved through the means of civil war, wrote Levien, the Moscow-born son of a German businessman. At first, Toller tried to give a firm but friendly rebuttal. In an article headlined "So much fuss over an omelette", he called Levien's attack a "literary polemic", and added that if this brief rebuttal was not enough for Herr

Levien, "then he may get a more thorough one from the communist masses, who have no desire to bring about a new split within the ranks of revolutionary workers".

But neither Max Levien nor his party comrades were going to be content with such a flippant dismissal of this central issue. He and the editors of the *Rote Fahne*, who answered to Eugen Leviné, stood their ground and insisted that the question of violence was a central one. No one who rejected violence would be able to carry out a successful revolution.

But Toller wouldn't budge from his position, either. He didn't "see every member of the bourgeoisie as a murderer, looter and robber", though he also pleaded for people to combat the Establishment "and those who consciously represent it all the more fiercely", and "to ally the struggle of hate to the struggle of love".

Sincerely bewildered, he wrote: "Levien is scornfully rejecting the hand of brotherhood which we extend to the communist masses, so that we may work together." And he ended his disappointed article, which appeared in the *Neue Zeitung* on 29th March, with the words: "It is ridiculous to turn an alliance between parties into a reason for a malicious attack, if the policy, will and actions of the other party are all aimed at the same *goals*! The parties in their current form are all on their deathbeds. Only socialism will live, only the revolutionary man will live."

Yes, the young poet Ernst Toller feels the wind beneath his wings. A mighty wind. In these days, it sweeps him through the revolutionary city. He loves these people, the preachers, the saviours, everyone who sees the end of the war as more of a liberation than a defeat. As the start of something new, something unprecedented. As if they had heard what he'd called out to them in his play *Transformation*: "And you could all be human beings, if you just believed in yourselves and in mankind, if you were replete in your spirit."

And how replete with spirit Munich is now. How ready to reinvent the people, the city. Or the world. "The way! The way! Thou poet, show us," the people begged in his play. Now, he is ready.

But first he wants to go to Berlin. To an Independent Social Democrat conference. He wants to report on the progress he has made down here in Bavaria, to spread euphoria and request support for all that is about to happen. He was planning to take the train to Berlin, but the Central Council's final session of the day has gone on for ever once again. Very well then, he'll fly, the next morning, 4th April. It's his first ever flight.

The pilot is already waiting. He's a fighter pilot, with an Iron Cross First Class and a gold squadron badge pinned to his uniform. The sky is a Mediterranean blue and Toller sits behind the pilot. He watches the ground receding through a square hole from which, until a few months ago, bombs fell to earth. Toller marvels like a child: "The black forests, green fields, brown hills and ravines become neat, flat, coloured squares from a toy-box, bought in a department store and fitted together by a little boy's hands. Great mountains of cloud rise up around me. The earth is soon veiled in a soft white layer of mist that exerts an uncanny pull, and the impulse to fling myself down and sink through it addles my senses."

Suddenly the plane starts to lose height, gliding and finally hurtling straight towards the ground and nose-diving into a field. The revolutionary poet hits his head on the inside of the fuselage and loses consciousness. When he comes to he learns that they have only got as far as Vilshofen, near Passau. The pilot flies the plane, which is only slightly damaged, back to Munich with Toller on board.

The next morning: a different plane, a different pilot. The second flight of Toller's life. He thinks of the day before. He straps himself in.

Minutes later they land roughly in a field of wet clay. Peasants who have watched the crash come rushing from all directions. They don't care about the two aviators in the wrecked plane. They have brought bottles, pans and buckets to collect the petrol flowing from the tank. "In those days, petrol was more precious than gold, more precious than life," writes Toller.

Still wearing their heavy flying suits, the poet and the pilot drag themselves to a tavern in a nearby village, lie down on the benches and fall asleep at once, "exhausted by the shock". They sleep for hours.

When Toller wakes up, he sees a policeman standing in the doorway. "No you don't, Frenchie," he says, and makes it clear to the victim of the plane crash that he is not permitted to leave the room. Toller, relieved that this is just a misunderstanding, explains: "I'm not a Frenchman."

As proof, he hands the policeman his revolutionary papers. The man looks at them and his eyes widen; he takes the plane passenger out into the corridor and says:

"So, Herr Toller, is it? Can't tell the peasants that, mind. They think you're a Frenchie, see, and if they knew you was a Red they'd kill you soon as look at you."

What can he do—the poet Toller, the head of Munich's USPD, who is so ready to show the people the way?

First he takes the narrow-gauge railway to Ingolstadt, hoping to get back to Munich from there. Is there another train to Munich today? he asks the stationmaster politely. There follows a swift back-and-forth, from a place where the revolution still has no reality. And Toller writes it up in *I Was a German*:

"Aye."

"I must take it, then."

"No you won't."

"Why not?"

"It's the Landtag train, it don't stop here."

"It has to stop."

"That train wouldn't stop here if you was the king of Bavaria."

"I'm not the king of Bavaria."

But he *is* the head of the Munich USPD. Once again he shows his papers, proudly, still hoping they will have the desired effect.

"Makes no odds to me, boy," says the stationmaster.

"I see," says Toller. He puts a hand in his pocket, grasping a handkerchief as if it's a revolver, and looking daggers at the stationmaster. "You *will* stop that train."

And it is this child's trick that actually performs the miracle. People here think the Reds from the city are contemptible buffoons all right, but buffoons who might also be dangerous. There have been a lot of stories about assassinations, robberies, savage dispossessions. So it's entirely possible that the hand in the pocket really is a gun.

"At your service, Herr Toller."

Ten minutes later the train stops, and Toller embarks and goes back to Munich. Nothing comes of the conference in Berlin. But king of Bavaria—that's a possibility.

Sunday, the 6th of April 1919, ten o'clock in the evening. The Wittelsbach palace, the queen's bedchamber. It has finally happened. Everyone is there. Representatives of the socialist parties, anarchist groups, representatives of the Workers' and

Soldiers' Councils, the Peasants' Council. Only the communists are absent. And the scouts from the north of Bavaria. No matter. This is it. In the past few hours the Council Republic has been proclaimed in Würzburg, Augsburg, Fürth, Aschaffenburg, Lindau, Hof. There's actually nothing more to discuss. The palace is ready. Toller's eyes roam the assembly. "Where ladies-in-waiting and powdered lackeys once fawned and curtsied, workmen, farmers and soldiers now trudge in their heavy boots. Red Guards, couriers and bleary-eyed typists lean on the silk curtains at the windows of the ex-queen's bedroom."

As head of the Central Council, Ernst Niekisch opens the meeting. And they're off.

Gustav Landauer has waited a long time for this moment. Landauer, who wants to reshape the Bavarian soul. Eisner had brought him to Munich in November, but he was soon criticizing the Prime Minister for his willingness to compromise, and in the end he gave the eulogy at his old comrade's funeral. His moment has arrived. He has spent a long time hesitating, a long time waiting for this moment. When Ernst Toller sought him out in 1917, in the town of Krumbach in Bavarian Swabia, and asked Landauer to join him in the great struggle against the war, to fight for a new peace, a good peace, he told the young hothead: "I have spent my whole life working to see this society crumble, a society built on lies and deception, on exploitation and suppression, and now I know it will, tomorrow or in a year's time, I have the right and the breath to save myself for this time. When the hour is at hand, I will be there and I will work."

Now that hour has come. There is no doubt about it. In the last few days, Landauer and Erich Mühsam have retreated to a restaurant to draft a proclamation for the Council Republic. "To the people of Bavaria," they wrote at the top of the paper, and underlined the words. Then just one sentence on the next line: "The decision has been made."

Landauer has the paper in his hand. He is a tall man, who towers over the whole assembly. Proud, thin, bearded, upright, he looks like a new, elongated Kurt Eisner. He knows exactly what needs to be done. He proposes that those present declare themselves the constitutive assembly of the Bavarian Council Republic. "He said that revolution has always been a creative act, which must begin with an unexpected step," Niekisch later recalls. Then there are more speeches and discussions, people making the same arguments again and again.

But something is different that night. Over the course of the day, all the ministers in the ministerial council led by Johannes Hoffmann have stepped down. There is now officially a vacuum at the top of the state. And Landauer is so clear and so resolute. No one votes against his motion. Niekisch is the only one to abstain.

After everyone has talked over each other for a while, they move on to the distribution of offices in this future Council Republic. The ministers won't be called ministers any longer; they will be "people's delegates". First, they need to appoint a foreign minister, or rather a "People's Delegate for Foreign Affairs". Erich Mühsam takes the floor, says a few words about himself, points out his popularity abroad, his good relationship with the communists—in short, he knows who the most suitable candidate for the job is: him.

An awkward silence in the queen's bedchamber. Niekisch writes: Mühsam "was an effervescent, witty soul, a good man, but such a literary bohemian that no one could imagine him in a dignified official post".

Well. What to do? Someone has to say something. His friend Landauer, who just a few days previously drew up the council resolution with him, breaks the silence. Erich knows, he says, just how devoted Landauer is to him, and he is most certainly suitable and usable for any office he cares to name. But for this important post he lacks "the experience, the mastery of the apparatus, the sure-footedness required for diplomatic negotiation". He is sorry, Landauer says, but he has to speak against him as a candidate. Then Toller jumps in. He agrees with Landauer: Mühsam is not the right man for the job. Instead someone proposes a man named Franz Lipp for this high office. Niekisch will later claim it was Toller who brought this gentleman into play. Toller disputes that claim vociferously.

Very well then: Herr Lipp. No one knows him, no one knows what he can do. Ernst Toller says of him: "His face was all beard; his suit nothing but a frock coat, and these two requisites seemed to be the only things that made him eligible for the position. A worker whom I asked about Dr Lipp said that he was a personal friend of the Pope's."

All right, that will have to do. There are other posts to give out. Niekisch, who is still head of the Central Council and chair of this meeting, writes with some surprise: "The person earmarked for the transport office was Georg Paulukun, who was quite clearly a vagrant." The home affairs job goes to a gentleman known for his never-ending speeches. Agriculture "was taken by Kübler, a fanatical member of the Peasants' League", and defence is cheerfully handed to a man called Reichert, "a former waiter of unmistakable deviousness", according to Ernst Niekisch.

And so they continue into the night, happily forming a Bavarian cabinet of dreamers in the queen's bedchamber. It seems anyone can become a people's delegate today, except Erich Mühsam.

And then Eugen Leviné's arrival is announced. Finally! The communist! What would a council republic be without the members of the official Communist Party? It was clear, of course, that on this night of power they would ultimately join the government.

But Leviné has other ideas. He comes in wearing his flat cap, black suit, his large eyes under hooded lids, cool and determined. No one should be surprised by his appearance here, he says. He has been saying it ever since he arrived in Munich, aloud and in writing, clearly and forcefully: revolution means violence. Revolution means overturning the whole of society. Revolution knows no compromise, no give and take, no mercy for anyone. Only today, on 6th April, they could all have read as much in the *Rote Fahne*, where he described the previous meeting, the unsuccessful proclamation of the Bavarian Council Republic: "This society wants to found a council republic? Yes, this society wants it, believes it wants it, or gives the appearance of wanting it. We hold our heads in our hands. Are we dreaming? Has the world gone mad? It would be ridiculous, comic, grotesque, were it not such a damned serious business."

Leviné explains that the Council Republic, if that really is what they are proclaiming here, is a "pseudo-council republic" that makes a mockery of the noble name. They, the communists, want no part in it and he strongly advises them against proclaiming anything. And then he's gone.

Silence in the bedchamber.

How is this going to work—a council republic without the communists? With resistance from the communists, even? Really, it's out of the question. But what to do? Call Leviné back? Plead with him one more time? Call the whole thing off? Go home without having formed a new republic?

Niekisch asks the assembly to consider whether this new state of affairs should alter their decision. The individual parties and groups withdraw to talk among themselves. The Social Democrats have now lost all enthusiasm for the project. But no one dares say that.

Then they reconvene. None of the groups sees a reason to change anything about the new government they are planning. No one wants to admit they're dependent on the communists. So there are no communists there. That's fine. They'll be able to govern that much more easily and peaceably.

Secretly disheartened, publicly undeterred, they press on. There are still a few "people's commissariats" to distribute. First: finance. Wham: a hand shoots up. It belongs to the businessman and financial theorist Silvio Gesell, another man with a huge beard and dark circles around his eyes. Like Landauer, he too has waited many, many years for this moment. He knows how to reform the financial world. He knows how to do away with interest. He knows how to keep money constantly on the move, circulating, working for the workers, not the capitalists who hoard it. With him in charge, with his theory of "free money", they will see interest vanish from the world for all time. He can't believe that his global formula has been semi-ignored for so long. Immediately after the Russian Revolution he had written a letter to Comrade Lenin. "Dear Comrade, a revolution that brings privations for the people is certain to fail," he had written. "Our free money would now give quite an extraordinary stimulation to work, since it ensures the exchange of products under any and all circumstances; this system alone will guarantee everyone the full proceeds of their personal labour. Free money would quite automatically set this labour on the right track." And, since this is not the time for theorizing, he suggests sending a suitable person to St Petersburg at their own expense to give Comrade Lenin a personal lecture on the system and provide him with "the necessary instructions for implementing the reform". Unfortunately, the letter came back to Gesell unopened.

Well then, he'll do it here in Bavaria. Gesell has been a businessman in Argentina, a farmer in Switzerland, and at one time lived in the idyllic vegetarian colony of Eden, north of Berlin. For thirty years, he explains, he has gone to bed every night fearing that he might die without the world having taken up his treasure, his interest secret. His theory is very simple. Money, as Gesell wishes it to be, loses value within a very short space of time. And that means it is spent quickly, stimulates the economy, and prevents people from hoarding capital. They will no longer be slaves to interest. Money will be subject to a weekly tax, and banknotes will be stamped when the tax is paid. Unstamped notes will be rejected by the state coffers.

He will also introduce basic pensions for mothers. For the transition period, there will be a wealth tax on fortunes over 10,000 marks, staggered according to the amount. Anything over 300,000 marks will be confiscated. Private ownership of land will be abolished. In the long term, it will be abolished all over the world. "The earth belongs to mankind!" he explains. "It must be declared the inalienable property of the people. The natural resources, the coal seams, the potash mines do not belong to individual nations. There is no English coal, no German potash, no Romanian petrol." The treasures of the earth belong "in their entirety to all people".

But above all and before anything else, there must be an end to hoarding money. Immediately. The money squirrel is the most dangerous animal of all, Silvio Gesell is convinced. Money has to flow, to stream, to be transformed into goods, into happiness. Immediately. And he will force money into a fluid state quickly, as quickly as Silvio Gesell wants. He has an array of splendid images to describe it. His theory is not a theory. His theory is pure practice: "picture this: money will rot like potatoes, pollute the air like guano, explode like dynamite, be fed like a horse, operated like machinery. It will take up space like cotton, weigh heavy like bricks, corrode like sulphuric acid, shatter like glass."

Explode! Shatter! Corrode! Silvio Gesell becomes the People's Delegate for Finance.

Finally, there is the post of People's Delegate for Education and Public Instruction. Landauer's mission in life. Reshaping souls! It wasn't Eisner who had thought up this task. It was Gustav Landauer's great goal to reshape people's souls from the ground up. New thinking. New hearts. Starting in the schools. Continuing the work in the universities. The plan, his plan for government, has been ready and waiting for a long time. All the essays he's written about literature, about Goethe, Hölderlin, Walt Whitman, Leo Tolstoy, his lectures on Shakespeare—at bottom they were all mental preparation for this. The transformation of the idea into reality.

Gustav Landauer has found everything in the works of his masters. In the past, for the present. "Goethe desired nothing so much as to be *realized*... the fact that the greatest of his works have such a compelling power and move us in the real sense of the word, comes from this urge for realization: he would so have loved to pour it into men's shattered hearts, but he had to load it into his literary works."

It is now up to him, Landauer, to release the spirit of these great works of humanity into the real world. Johann Wolfgang von Goethe, as Gustav Landauer read him, had always had in mind this night, the approaching dawn of this republic.

"It is time!" Landauer liked to say, quoting from Goethe's "Fairy Tale". "We are met at a fortunate hour; let each fulfil his office, let each discharge his duty; and a general happiness will alleviate each individual trouble."

And here in this room, Gustav Landauer is also one of the few who is heartily glad that the communists have rejected them. His book *For Socialism*, which everyone is reading in these days, which even Thomas Mann has read with great interest, is above all a polemic against dogmatic Marxism and in favour of the immediate realization of living, flowing socialism. He had written: "What the nationalistic bourgeois has made of the German students, the Marxists have made of broad segments of the proletariat, cowardly little men without youth, wildness, courage, without joy in attempting anything, without sectarianism, without heresy, without originality and individuality. But we need all that. We need attempts. We need the expedition of 1,000 men to Sicily. We need these precious Garibaldi-natures, and we need failures upon failures and the tough nature that is frightened by nothing, that holds firm and endures and starts over and over again until it succeeds, until we are through, until we are unconquerable."

And now the time has come. The culmination of a lifetime of thinking, reading and planning. It is the night of realization. He has found these three questions and answers in Leo Tolstoy. Fundamental rules for life. "What time is the most important? What person? What soul? Time—the present moment; person—the one you currently have to do with; soul—the salvation of one's own soul, meaning the work of love."

Landauer is ready for the office of People's Delegate for Education and Public Instruction. And now, with the communists on the outside, his appointment will be a mere formality. But then someone else speaks up, someone from the Peasants'

League. He has reservations, he says. Serious reservations. Landauer is a Jew, an aesthete, he's not Bavarian. He doesn't know if this man can communicate with the rural, Catholic population out there. They'd be making the whole of the new government unnecessarily vulnerable to attack if they entrusted such an important office to a man like Landauer. He's thinking of Eisner, he says, who looked so like this man, who *was* so like him, and who was equally out of place in the countryside.

These reservations seem to convince a few people. Landauer hesitates. Can this be happening? Is it really possible now? Being a Jew, not being a Bavarian: are these genuine arguments against him at this hour?

Then Erich Mühsam speaks. The friend whom Landauer has just robbed of the Foreign Ministry. Yes, Landauer rejected him. But he wants to speak up for Landauer. The arguments of the Peasants' League, Mühsam shouts, are objections from a bygone, pre-revolutionary age. Revolution means they need new methods, new points of view, new men. Anyone who takes exception to foreign aesthetes and Jews is a reactionary. There Mühsam ends, and Gustav Landauer becomes a people's delegate.

Carried forward by their enthusiasm, they now move on to the proclamation of the republic. The text already exists: the Mühsam-Landauer resolution from the restaurant. While they are working on the final phrasing, telegrams go out to every district authority in the state, announcing Bavaria's transformation into a council republic and, at Landauer's personal request, instructing that the church bells be rung in celebration. The telegrams all bear the signature of Ernst Niekisch, the head of the Central Council. He will later claim never to have placed it there. He will begin to regard the whole thing as rather sinister. This isn't poetry any longer: it's politics now. It's reality.

Someone pesters Landauer to include the words "class struggle" in the proclamation. He erupts. "Four years!" he cries. "The German people spent four years in a murderous frenzy. Are we to continue that frenzy? Is our task not to become sober, to become human again?" Landauer himself looks frenzied. They leave him to get on with his work.

Meanwhile, Toller is engaged in his own struggle. He is writing up the conditions formulated by his party, the USPD, in the course of the night's negotiations: they plan to publish them the next day, along with a statement that their conditions have been accepted. These conditions actually comprise all the demands that the Communist Party would make of a council republic. Toller wants to shield himself and the new government from the outset against accusations from the communists that the republic they have founded on this night is only a pseudo-council republic. Their demands include a "dictatorship of the class-conscious proletariat"; the "introduction of a universal obligation to work, including for the bourgeoisie"; an "alliance with the Soviet Republics of Russia and Hungary"; and the "right to asylum for political refugees from all countries, meaning a refusal to enforce arrest warrants". And Toller adds: "Since our communist conditions have been accepted, and in view of the enormous responsibility involved, we agree to join the government."

Finally all the declarations and proclamations are ready. "To the people of Bavaria!" the official proclamation begins. "The decision has been made. Bavaria is a Council Republic." At Landauer's suggestion, a national holiday has been called in this new state. "As a sign of our joyful hope for a bright future for the whole of mankind", there will be no work on the first day of the new republic. It is the 7th of April. Gustav Landauer's birthday. The whole city will celebrate.

Then, at last, they hold a ballot. There are no votes against. Ernst Niekisch is the only one to abstain. The Bavarian Council Republic is proclaimed. Ernst Niekisch stands down as president of the Central Council; later, Ernst Toller will be named as his successor. And with that, Toller is the new head of government.

The goal, the dream, the utopia, have become reality.

A new day. A new state.

Ernst Niekisch writes: "It was six in the morning before the negotiations reached an end. Tired, I returned from the meeting to the hotel. I was under the impression that I had been involved in a political grotesque. Now, in the grey light of dawn, the farcical events of the night just past lost all their cheerful, conciliatory colour; they appeared with a shrill, stinging nakedness as what they were: political facts that could not fail to have serious consequences."

Ernst Toller writes: "As I leave the Wittelsbach palace the new day is dawning. The revolution is an established fact. But— is it? This Council Republic is a foolish *coup de main* by the bewildered workers, an attempt to salvage the lost revolution.

What will it achieve? How will it end?

One of our section leaders is waiting outside the little hotel where I am staying.

'We've got power now,' he says.

'Have we?' I reply. He looks taken aback by that, stares at me thoughtfully, and I hasten to take my leave."

The previous day, the inhabitants of the villa on the Herzogpark had also guessed that a council republic would be declared. All the same, Thomas Mann was a little unsettled. He wrote a note to his friend Ernst Bertram, asking if he would come over. The children took the note to him and he, the good fellow, came at once.

Thomas Mann lay down on his chaise longue, and Bertram read aloud to him from a little-known essay by Adalbert Stifter about the solar eclipse on 8th July 1842. "There are things that one knows for fifty years, and in the fifty-first year one marvels at their gravity and dreadfulness," Stifter's essay begins. And Thomas Mann, who on the night of 7th November pointed out the "beauty of the damp, starry sky" as they walked home and explained that the eternal put him in a contemplative mood, listens attentively to his friend.

It is the story of an apocalypse. It is only the sun that has gone, but suddenly it feels as if they have lost everything: "Our shadows lay empty and insubstantial against the wall; our faces were ashen—this slow death in the midst of the morning freshness we had enjoyed until just a few minutes ago. We had imagined the eclipse as like the fall of evening, for instance, only without a sunset; but we had not imagined the spectral quality of an evening without a sunset," Ernst Bertram reads to his good friend. He reads of the one moment of total darkness, when a unanimous "Ah" comes from every mouth, "and then a deathly silence. It was the moment when God spoke and mankind listened."

Bertram reads and reads; he reads about the "silent majesty", the moment when people sense that God must be present now if ever He was, the moment in which the people try to put what they have experienced into words again, as they always put everything into words, wanting to capture happiness and unhappiness, but at that very moment, just before the first word is spoken, it passes. The darkness has passed, the end of the world. The old world that they knew from all the years before is back, but it is new, transformed. For one eerie moment they saw it perish and disappear. They have experienced the transformation and now they are themselves transformed. Ernst Bertram goes on reading to his friend on the chaise longue: "We looked each other in the eye—and one victorious sunbeam followed another, and how narrow, how vanishingly narrow that shining circle was at first. It was as though we were being given an ocean of light—one cannot say it, and anyone who has not experienced it will hardly believe what a joyous, triumphant relief entered our hearts: we shook hands and said that all our lives, we would remember having seen this together."

After the reading, the friends talk about frightening natural phenomena, then about political and literary matters. Until night finally falls. They take a late supper and Thomas Mann notes: "We ate baked fish, goose schmaltz, oranges and sweetmeats. A pleasant evening, with the sword of Damocles of the Commune and dispossession hanging over us."

The next morning, Bavaria wakens as a Council Republic. The weather is mild and damp. The editorial offices of the *Münchner Neueste Nachrichten* have been occupied by the new rulers. Landauer's proclamation is splashed across the front page. It also appears on posters plastered all over the city. Munich is quiet on this drizzly new public holiday. Landauer's forty-ninth birthday.

That morning, he proudly sends a telegram to his two daughters, who are staying with relatives outside the city— Landauer's wife died the previous year. "On my birthday Council Republic is proclaimed today is national holiday I am People's Delegate for Education and Public Instruction, previously culture minister. Warmest wishes your father."

He sends a postcard to a friend with a portrait of himself on it. Again, he writes that his birthday is a public holiday, outlines his new area of responsibility and adds, wavering between hope and melancholy: "If they give me a few weeks, I hope to achieve something; however, it is quite possible that it will only be a few days, and then all this will have been but a dream."

But for now, the first task is to move into the Wittelsbach palace. Which rooms there will suit their needs? The new people's delegates and their friends and comrades roam the corridors. Journalists, including many from foreign papers, have come to learn about the new situation. An American from Chicago, Ben Hecht, has just arrived by plane from Berlin, travelling, or so he claims, with a Bolshevist carrying a million gold marks in his suitcase and with several anti-Bolshevists, all intending to support their various movements here in Munich.

Hecht can't stop laughing and gaping incredulously at this fairy-tale land of so-called revolutions. His articles are full of ridicule and disbelief, but also some sympathy for what he sees here in Munich. Maybe he invents some things as well. Maybe the whole enterprise seems so unreal to him that he thinks no one will notice if he embellishes it a little.

Hecht is there when Ernst Toller is looking for office space—or at least, he writes about it. Hecht says that a friend, the poet "Rudy Hise" from Frankfurt, is advising Toller as he searches. This Rudy carries a carbine and a bayonet; half a dozen hand grenades dangle from his belt, and he explains to the American reporter that the little bottle he has about his person is filled with "pure nitroglycerin". It's enough to blow up the whole palace. And by the way, he is the head of the Committee for Public Safety. When Ben Hecht asks him what responsibilities this entails, he proudly declares: "We take care of traitors, cowards and saboteurs. We liquidate them."

It seems that even serious American reporters allow themselves to be infected by the poetic revolution. In any case, there is no mention of a Frankfurt poet named Rudy Hise in the annals of German literature.

So, Ben Hecht is now on the hunt for a suitable office with Ernst Toller and a fictitious bomber-poet. They visit a high-ceilinged hall. "Too big," whispers Rudy. "The workers would not like such ostentation."

On they go through the palace. "Toller, the dictator of Bavaria since noon, paused in a doorway. 'This will do,' he said. We entered a commodious bathroom. In a corner was an oversized zinc tub. The floor was covered with worn linoleum. 'We will use this as our headquarters,' said Toller. 'Have some workmen board over the bathtub and bring a big table and some chairs in.' The new government agreed. They would find cubbyholes of their own in the palace, but this bathroom would be the headquarters of Herr Toller, Bavaria's new dictator."

Ernst Toller describes his first moments as the head of Bavaria's government rather differently. First and foremost, he learnt what it meant to head a cabinet in this age. An age after the great, lost war with all its casualties. An age of hunger, poverty, a tremendous sense of defeat and at the same time tremendous hope. He learnt what it meant to be the man on whom all hopes were pinned. The dream-realizer for all the dreamers who were relying on him. On him and his new government. And the government had fed that hope with all their talk of salvation and love and great unity and the fulfilment of wishes. The palace very quickly filled with people: those whom Toller had brought to tears with his speeches had come to demand that he and his government solve their problems, fulfil their dreams.

Munich, capital of the south, a city of people seeking happiness, salvation and utopia. And all of them, so it seemed to Toller, had now found their way into his new palace, to have their own small, private utopias realized by their magical king:

People crowd the ante-rooms of the Central Council, each one of them believing that the Council Republic has been expressly created to satisfy his own private desires. A woman wants to get married at once; there have been some difficulties, as she lacked the necessary papers, but obviously the Council Republic could now salvage her personal happiness. A man wants me to force his landlord to remit his rent. A group of revolutionary citizens has come to demand the arrest of all their personal enemies, former skittles partners and clubmen.

Unappreciated reformers submit their programmes for the betterment of humanity, believing that at last their ideas, scorned for decades, will have a chance to turn earth into Paradise. They each have their own specific panacea; and, granted their premises, their logic is unimpeachable. Some believe that the root of all evil is eating cooked food, others the gold standard, others non-porous underwear, or working with machinery, or the lack of a compulsory universal language and universal shorthand, or department stores and sex education. They all remind me of the Swabian shoemaker who wrote a voluminous pamphlet to prove that man owed his moral sickness to the fact that he satisfied his elementary needs in closed rooms and with the aid of artificial paper. If he spent these minutes out in the woods and availed himself of the natural moss, all spiritual poisons would also evaporate into the cosmos, and he would be purified in both body and spirit, returning to his work with his social conscience reinforced and his egotism diminished; true love of humanity would be awakened and the long-promised Kingdom of God on Earth would be at hand.

Thus reads Toller's report on the Council Republic's office of dreams. But now: fantasists out! Work in! Toller has to govern. He has to implement his own plans and those of his comrades—and with great haste. Landauer is right. "It is very likely that it will only be a few days, and then all this will have been but a dream." Toller also knows this only too well. Their opponents are everywhere: on the left, the right, in the centre ground, on the streets. Yes, he feels buoyed up by the massed workers, he knows that he stands for what is right. But he's also despondent. He is starting to realize that he has done the wrong thing. That going ahead and founding a communist republic against the wishes of the communists is a doomed enterprise. But then, here he is, sitting in his palace. And the government is governing. It's what he has been fighting and writing and speaking for all this time.

But it is only midday on his first day of government when news reaches them that a group of armed students and soldiers has gathered at the university to march on the Wittelsbach palace. At once, panic breaks out. Alarmed stenographers rush out of the building; functionaries stride around, pale with fear. But Ernst Niekisch, the former head of the Central Council, who has come to the seat of government for an orderly handover, is astonished at his successors' apparent courage. "Landauer and Mühsam behaved surprisingly well. Joining forces with a number of workers, they went to the cupboards and fetched machine guns, hand grenades and other weapons, and readied themselves for battle. They were determined to repel the attack or die in the attempt. I walked through the rooms, reassuring people and telling them it would not be as bad as it seemed."

It wasn't bad at all. No students and soldiers had gathered, or at least, none who intended to storm the palace. It was just one of a thousand rumours that buzzed around the city in these days, each of them believed by someone.

At first, public speeches help to quell the rumours, and the government maintains a presence in the city, in the beer cellars, the assembly halls. Ernst Toller goes out on his very first day of government: that afternoon he is in the Hofbräuhaus, where the Munich factory councils, workers' committees and the Munich Workers' Council have gathered. Toller has to explain, placate, enthuse, all at once. And unite the workers, despite the absurd squabbles between their leaders. It's the only way to give him and his republic a chance. Toller, the polemicist: "Hard work and the travails of everyday life have made us brothers. It now falls to us to stand shoulder to shoulder against the capitalist class. We have no time to lose.

Put yourselves above all leaders if they are opposed to the unity of the whole proletariat. Our task is not to pander to the vanity of leaders but to alleviate the hardships of the proletariat."

Toller warns, Toller praises, Toller sympathizes, Toller waxes euphoric. He says he wants to give the workers the excess of living space, food and clothing that the rich possess. He explains that he is constantly receiving messages from rural areas saying that the brothers there stand with them. That the whole of Western Europe will soon be marching alongside them, too. That their suffering in the war has not been in vain. That now their moment has come, and unity in the struggle against the capitalists is crucial. He warns against people who call on the workers to commit atrocities. The reason Bavaria has forged ahead so successfully in the proletarian struggle is that so far, all violence has been avoided. "Proletarian blood must be sacred to us at all times."

Pugnaciously, he bends the truth into shape. He needs to know whom he has taken on this fight for. He now needs a sense of unity, of euphoria. Against the people out there who run everything down, against the envious, the nay-sayers, the mockers, the opponents on all sides.

Everything he demands, everything he promises and announces is accepted unanimously on this afternoon in the Hofbräuhaus. The workers here are proud of their republic and their new people's king with his infectious enthusiasm.

Perhaps they also sense the bind that he and his government are in. The government led by Prime Minister Hoffmann has now fled to Bamberg and is under the protection of a newly formed volunteer militia, the Epp Freikorps. They have arrested people acting for the Council Republic in Franconia, and they control northern Bavaria. And at some point, when they feel strong enough and have gathered enough Freikorps soldiers, they will march south to their lost capital—that much is certain.

At the same time, communists everywhere are agitating against Toller and his councils. They call the workers out to demonstrations and send speakers into the barracks to announce that this Council Republic does not deserve to be defended by soldiers.

None of this helps. Now they just have to screw up their courage and keep looking straight ahead. Toller writes decrees, flyers, permits. An appeal against anti-Semitic agitation warns of "reactionary conspirators who want to goad the masses into Jewish pogroms, to clear the way for the Prussian Freikorps to enter Bavaria". Then he signs a "decree on the confiscation and rationing of living space". He may not have imagined himself having to devote his time to the conversion of rooms rather than the transformation of human beings, but that's how it is. Point four: "In communities with housing shortages, housing will be rationed. Space will be distributed as follows: single people will be allocated only one room plus kitchen, and for every family a minimal number of bedrooms and a living room. The number of bedrooms will be decided based on their size, as well as the number of family members and their age and sex." This decree alone has ten points, and anyone who doesn't comply is threatened with a 100,000-mark fine or up to a year in jail. "Avoidances are more difficult to penalize than direct contravention. Signed, Toller."

The author Ernst Toller has never written anything so practical, with such an immediate impact on life. And so it goes on. Decree after decree. One on general Sunday closing, in which he stipulates that from henceforth this also applies to the press, although "Grocers are exempt from this directive." Then the press is socialized, the eight-hour working day made legally binding, the mining industry is socialized. He decrees that citizens may only withdraw 100 marks per day from the banks, and jewels and other valuables may no longer be removed from safety-deposit boxes (which sends Thomas Mann's mother-in-law Hedwig Pringsheim, who has jewels worth 300,000 marks in the bank, into a panic, and causes her son-in-law to snigger in secret that she will probably "forfeit" her jewellery). And Toller goes on decreeing. After the bank and safe decree, he immediately issues a reassurance to the "workers and little people", saying that these measures of course do not affect them in any way, and that they shouldn't worry: "There are rumours that the savings of the workers and little people in building societies, co-operatives and banks are in danger. Do not believe these lies. The measures we have taken are directed against the major capitalists who are attempting to take money abroad." There follows a decree against exorbitant rents and one on the "distribution of studio spaces", which instructs that available studios "are only to be allocated to persons working primarily as artists, architects, photographers or in other professions to which a studio is absolutely necessary". Client politics. As head of state, Toller isn't just a friend to the workers, but also to the artists.

The most vital thing, however, is not to lose sight of the bigger picture. Toller orders the release of all prisoners of war, announces that a revolutionary tribunal will be set up, calls for the disarmament of the bourgeoisie and decides that wages will be paid on the new national holiday.

Of course Toller senses that he doesn't have much time. Of course he knows that he is presiding over a dream cabinet. Everything might vanish into thin air tomorrow, into thin air and blood. But he wants to gain people's confidence through work, through good deeds and fiery speeches.

One of the new government's first telegrams goes to Lenin, who replies at once, but also gives a few conditions that the new government will have to fulfil before it can be taken seriously as a genuine council government.

From the minute he takes office, the man so unexpectedly named as People's Delegate for Foreign Affairs, Dr Franz Lipp, does everything in his power to ensure that the new government is not taken seriously on the world stage. It may well be true that he is personally acquainted with the Pope.

He certainly sends him plenty of telegrams. His very first one goes to Vatican City: "I take it as my sacred duty to guarantee the safety of Your Holiness and the whole institution of the Nunciature in Munich. Have faith in my devotion."

The American journalist Ben Hecht is also taken aback by Dr Lipp. He reports that Lipp has cut all the phone lines in his office. He has a phobia of bells, Hecht says, and the sound of a telephone triggers a form of epilepsy.

But Lipp prefers sending telegrams to making phone calls in any case. After a while, an official from the telegraph office contacts Toller, asking whether he is really supposed to send everything the Delegate for Foreign Affairs wants to telegraph out to the world. They have just been given another telegram for the Pope in which Dr Lipp complains that Hoffmann, the head of government in exile, has taken the key to his ministry toilet with him to Bamberg, and that the republic is threatened by "Noske's hairy gorilla hands". The telegram closes with the line: "We want peace for ever."

Toller sighs. "Without a doubt, Lipp has gone mad. We decide to send him immediately to a sanatorium. To avoid a public sensation, he has to resign voluntarily."

But where is he? In the Foreign Ministry, the secretaries' desks are covered in red carnations. Lipp distributed the flowers at the start of work that morning. He himself has disappeared. Where is he? Writing more dispatches?

Finally, he is flushed out and sent to Toller, for the latter to convince this bearded, telegram-happy Foreign Minister to step down of his own accord. Lipp enters the room and immediately starts babbling: has Toller seen this rowing oar in the palace, the king's oar, and did he know that the king always took it into his giant bathtub to paddle as he bathed, and that he generally did more bathing than governing?

Very interesting, thank you for the information. The more important question is whether he, Lipp, submitted this telegram. Lipp reads it through carefully. Oh yes, he wrote that with his own hand.

Very well then. Unfortunately, he will have to step down. The letter of resignation has been prepared already, he just needs to put his signature at the bottom.

"Lipp rises from his chair, adjusts his grey frock coat, takes out a comb and with a practised hand rearranges his Henri Quatre beard; then, replacing his comb, he takes up the pen, leans for a moment on the desk, and murmurs sadly: 'Even this will I do for the revolution.'"

Lipp signs and leaves.

What happens next:

"That same afternoon he is back in the ministry, giving flowers to the typists and editing more telegrams. Good Samaritans remove him from his office."

The other people's delegates are busy, too. Silvio Gesell reorganizes his Finance Ministry in a terrific hurry. His priority is the swift introduction of free money. And of course, rumours instantly start circulating in the city that people's savings will now be confiscated or lose all value within a week.

Because no other rumour leads so quickly to general panic, Gesell adds a department for information to his ministry. You might just as well call it a department for pacification. "Not even the slightest thing must happen unless the whole population can get a clear overview of it," this department announces on the very first day of its existence. "This is the only way to avoid great hordes of agitated people crowding round the bank's counters, taking out paper money, every time there is some public disturbance."

Silvio Gesell wants to devote all his strength to this great task. But in a Finance Ministry, a new boss is immediately faced with a huge flood of duties. A ministerial aide, setting down an initial folder of documents that require Gesell's attention, is instructed to "take care of these bits and bobs yourself".

Gesell, meanwhile, sets out the principles for his period in office and his central project: "Since free money is the only way to achieve an absolute currency, since in any case free money provides a strong stimulus to the whole national economy, and finally, since in the long term free money causes the interest rate to fall automatically and salaries to rise correspondingly, free money can be the only option for the Council Republic."

Gesell also sends telegrams to important people. He transmits this information to the Reichsbank's board of directors, with a request: "I want to take radical measures to restructure the currency, departing from a systemless paper-money economy and moving over to an absolute currency, and I would like your views on this matter."

Gesell doesn't have long to wait for them. The president of the Reichsbank, von Hagenstein, only requires five words for his response: "I warn you against experimentation!" Very well. Then they'll do it without the Reichsbank.

His cabinet colleague Gustav Landauer is just as eager and restless in these days. He is constantly visiting the other government offices and, according to Ben Hecht: "As he strode through the palace he kept crying out: 'Here comes Landauer!'"

Hecht interviews him every day, fascinated by Landauer's eccentricity. "He would pause during his talk and call out his name in a sudden shout. The interviews were mainly discussions of Walt Whitman." The cornerstone of his education policy, according to Hecht, is that at the age of ten, every child should learn to recite Walt Whitman from memory.

Landauer loves Whitman. He loves his verses and his politics with all his heart. "Whitman", Landauer had said earlier, "has from his people the feeling that it is a new beginning, fresh barbarians created from a mix of ethnicities, who usher in a new phase of history."

It was Landauer's dream to begin a new phase of history here in the new Bavaria, as a "foreigner" (which was how people usually referred to him now), together with all the other "foreigners" and the native Bavarians. It seemed he had learnt everything from Whitman, even that "all great art must light the way for the nation", creating a sun that we simply need to follow. Love is the message; not an abstract, general love of mankind but concrete, real, present-day love. "Whitman embraced this cosmic love and this exuberance of feeling; only out of this chaos, this abyss of ardency, so he believed, could his new nation arise," said Gustav Landauer, the loving reader.

He has of course already worked out his plan for education and culture. He has considered everything in advance, always vaguely hoping that this moment would arrive. And now—"Here comes Landauer!"—he has a chance to implement his programme. For example: the immediate separation of Church and state. In architecture: "The new era of human history must find expression in the monuments and public buildings that will be erected from now on. State commissions. Painting and sculpture are to be incorporated into architecture."

Also: "New museum buildings", "state acquisitions", "National Theatre. Free entry", "Control of theatre programming by an academy". Schools: "Comprehensive school for children aged seven to thirteen. Emphasis on drawing and gymnastics", "no school desks. New textbooks." Then: "After the comprehensive school, either practical education in a training school or a commune from thirteen to fifteen (pupils—teachers—masters) or middle school."

Going into more detail, Landauer adds: "Schoolwork to be completed at home merely encourages laziness in teachers. It is to be abolished in every subject, including the learning of foreign languages." And: "Children should also be able to move about freely and informally during lessons. It does no harm at all if they stop taking part in the lesson for a while and occupy themselves with something else. It should also go without saying that there is no place in our system for the cane, for which Gotha's teachers are demonstrating in the year 1919 (!)."

Just like Rainer Maria Rilke, who at the start of the year had written: "It is with children that the future begins, and when has a world movement ever been so poised to begin?", Gustav Landauer wants to create the new world with new, little people. Starting in the schools.

Like his colleague Silvio Gesell, he has no desire to be shackled by any kind of bureaucracy while he is reshaping the world. He writes to his colleagues, who have evidently been piling up work samples, suggestions and urgent documents on Landauer's desk: "I beg your understanding: I will not and cannot spend my time on this in the current situation. The task at hand is the complete reshaping of all the public institutions that serve the mind. I cannot be a slave to things past and insubstantial, to the kind of weary activity that goes round in circles and moves nothing forward."

Yes, the department will now sometimes fall short in terms of consistency, "but colourfulness is not a failing to those for whom juridical and legislative thought is not the be-all and end-all".

"Difficulties with expertise", Landauer writes to his alarmed colleagues, "are nothing to do with me." Nor does he want to know anything about parliamentary legislation for his new initiatives. "That is why we are in the revolution; mankind needs a jolt from time to time, and it is our duty to the revolution to act in a revolutionary way."

And he provides a brief definition of what the new republic is and what it means: "Our Council Republic is to be understood as nothing other than that which lives in the mind and seeks to be realized, that which will take any opportunity to become reality."

Anyone who wants to be part of this great project, to plough all his strength into it, with joy and a firm resolve, should tell him so. Individually. "I will not accept a general declaration." Everyone! Join! In!

One of Landauer's most important colleagues was the revolutionary Ret Marut, who during the war had edited the polemical pacifist magazine *Der Ziegelbrenner*, writing all the articles himself. Marut was an invisible man. He never appeared in public. In later years he would publish extremely successful class-war adventure novels from all over the world under the name B. Traven, while living in exile in Mexico as an unrecognized phantom. Now, here, as a revolutionary in Bavaria, remaining invisible wasn't such an easy task. At an evening of readings in the Steinicke bookshop at the end of 1918, he had read from the *Ziegelbrenner* while sitting in complete darkness, the text in front of him illuminated only by a thin beam of light—until the evening was hijacked. Marut said: "The lights were turned on and now the 'gentlemen' tried to throw the reader off the podium by force." Marut, panicking about his lost anonymity, later claimed (as he had also announced in the programme) that it had only been an actor reading that evening. In the next issue of his one-man magazine he gave a report on the gate-crashed event, followed by an emphatic appeal under the headline: "The global revolution begins". "Hello, fellow humans!" he began. "Hello!" Marut explained that he belonged to no party, and indeed could never belong to a party, for he was a free man and would remain so. This was the noblest aim on earth: "To be allowed to be human! I want to be free! I want to be joyful! I want to rejoice in all the beauty of this world! I want to be blissful! But my freedom is only assured if all the people around me are free." This piece appeared in the issue published at the end of January. It closed with a warning: "Movement. Come together! Do not fall asleep! The revolution has only just begun."

Now, in the Council Republic, the invisible opponent of the bourgeois press is in his element. He even attends a meeting of the Central Office for Economic Affairs on 8th April, quite un-anonymously, and on the same day presents a "plan for socializing the press" to a meeting of press representatives. He suggests that once all the newspapers have been socialized, the same process should be applied to "all the printing and publishing houses, the communication and news bureaus, paper factories, type foundries, theatres, cinemas". The current owners are to be expropriated without compensation. And he adds: "Those newspapers and magazines that are necessary must be run with public funds. The people will decide what is necessary." A state press governed by public law, which will also see to it that writers and journalists are properly remunerated: "The newspapers must immediately call on all writers and scholars to send in political, academic and technical essays. The work must be paid decently by the paper that accepts it."

Yes, Marut was another person who had waited a long time for this glorious moment in Bavaria. Like many other left-wing revolutionaries of the time, he too had railed against the lying wartime press, the bourgeois capitalist press that hid the truth about the capitalists' protection of their vested interests. The hatred for the bourgeois papers was boundless.

And the invisible man of letters Marut was their greatest enemy. He wrote himself hoarse: "Proletarians! The press is overdue for socialization; it must be liberated from profiteering businessmen. The press must be as free as schools are from business profits. No capitalist should earn money from the work of bringing knowledge and enlightenment to the people. The press should be a cultural institution, not a business. It should serve humanity, not lies and rabble-rousing. It should be an organ of truth in the hands of honourable intellectual workers. Revolutionary proletarians, I call on you to create this press!"

Another newspaper worker slept through the proclamation of the Council Republic. Oskar Maria Graf had been out in Nymphenburg, drinking at the Dutchman's house late into the night. A few days previously, at Graf's suggestion, they had put up a sign reading "Neutral Council Republic", so that no one would disturb their drinking sessions with the millionaire.

But now, on the morning of 8th April, his lover Marietta is shouting, "Graf! Graaaaf!" from the other end of the house. The painter Davringhausen joins the cry: "Oskar Maria! Come quickly, quickly!"

Yes, yes, all right. He's coming. They're being too loud. It's too early. Graf needs time. There is a copy of the *Münchner Neueste Nachrichten* on the breakfast table. "We've got a council republic," Marietta says succinctly. Graf skims the page and cries out: "I have to get there right away!"

And he rushes off, with Davringhausen at his side. There are no trams running. They stride through the fields, the sky a wonderful spring blue now that the rain has stopped.

They arrive at the Landtag bathed in sweat. The place is buzzing with rumours. Counter-revolutionary troops are on the march. Fear. Panic. Headless chickens. The two men carry on to the meeting hall of the Artists' Council, which is filled to bursting with the revolutionary artists of the moment: Alfred Wolfenstein, Georg Kaiser, and Graf's friends Schorsch Schrimpf, Ado von Achenbach and Bruno Tautz. Ado von Achenbach, "an idle, wool-gathering, literary aristocrat from Berlin", drags Graf back outside. They've made him the censor for the *Bayerische Kurier*, he says, and he can't do it alone. Graf has to help him. He's the ideal man.

Graf lets himself be dragged. Achenbach is euphoric and has brought with him a lengthy article he's written. "This has to go in today's paper," he cries as they arrive at the *Kurier*. "It can be the leading article in today's edition." Graf is instantly bored and wonders whether the new republic might not have more interesting, more controversial tasks for him.

Then an editor comes in, accompanied by a priest, both red in the face, flustered, angry. They have read the article, they say, and it can't be printed: the writing offends their religious sensibilities and will offend those of their readers. Achenbach retorts that they can moan as much as they like, these are the orders from the Central Council and they must comply. He himself will take full responsibility.

But the two men are not so easily convinced. It violates the freedom of religion, they say. They talk, complain, insist that the text cannot be printed. Finally they demand to speak to the People's Delegate for Education and Public Instruction, Landauer: "If our negotiations with him are fruitless, we will step down and leave everything to you."

Achenbach smiles and hesitates a moment. Graf leaps up, furious. "What? What is this? Hell's teeth, good God, what liberties are these!" he shouts. And then his shout swells into a sermon against false Catholicism, bigotry, the link between Church and state, the war. Graf is beside himself: "In wartime you had to print all the lies Ludendorff ordered you to," he shouts. "In wartime you preached that it was God's will for men to be killed! In wartime you printed every lie going! And now all at once you've rediscovered your faith! You're Catholics, are you?... So am I! But I've never seen anything so rotten and false! You yourselves are the greatest Pharisees!... I'm not having any of it! This article will be printed and no one is going to Landauer! There will be no negotiating! Government is government!"

The gentlemen from the *Bayerische Kurier* are appalled. They turn to Achenbach—this wild man is spouting blasphemies; he has to do something about it. Graf rages ever more shrilly, telling them to be quiet or he'll have them arrested. "Make a telephone call and have them seized at once!" Graf instructs Achenbach, the censor. But Achenbach doesn't make a telephone call.

Time passes. Everyone is silent. Graf looks out of the window. The atmosphere is tense. Then the two Catholics start up again, saying they really would like to see Landauer now. And Achenbach says all right, fine.

Graf gets up. He can't believe it. "You're the biggest fool there is," he tells Achenbach, and leaves.

Oskar Maria Graf walks through the city, the capital of the Council Republic. Saying nothing. At a loss. He sees the communist Max Levien giving a speech on the plinth of the Schiller monument in Maximilianplatz, accompanied by Napoleonic gesturing: death sentences, opening the safety-deposit boxes, big, big words. Graf can't help laughing. This revolution is all talk. A joke.

He goes home. Writes a letter to his Black Girl, starting it over and over again. World-weariness, longing, depression. A man lurches through the revolution he has dreamt of, which now is so unreal, so foolish, so false. "I don't know what I am or where I belong," he writes. "But I sometimes feel that the others aren't much different from me." It's funny, he writes, but when he reads the newspapers from northern Germany, where they are always writing about civil war in Munich, about "unscrupulous rabble-rousers, perpetrating unprecedented acts of terrorism with the aid of a fanatical minority"—it's all nonsense. "In reality everyone is just perpetually impatient for peace," he writes. And: "What a terrible, slimy, hellish tool the press is!"

There is certainly no civil war, "and most of the people in charge here are actually very fearful. They are afraid on two counts, one being their fear of the masses, which is why they are always talking themselves into greater radicalism, and the other the fear of their own courage. Nothing has happened to anyone here yet."

When he walks the city streets, he feels like he's in the fairy-tale land of Schilda, in the Empire of Utopia, where people try to shovel sunlight into a bucket to make a dark world glow. But it doesn't glow. The sun shines where it wants to.

"It's ludicrous, but it's human. It is so human that all

humans have lost respect for it. And that will help to snuff out this revolution, for the petty officers will never be wiped out."

But Graf now knows where he belongs. He walks back along the field path, out of the city, to the drinker's paradise in Nymphenburg. Has he been made a minister? the Dutchman asks him sarcastically. Oskar Maria Graf replies: "Me?... No, I'm staying here as your court jester."

A jester in a joke of a city.

But Graf was always ready with the most biting ridicule when it came to the outlandish saints who settled in Munich in these days. Like poor Gusto Gräser, who heeded the call of this buoyant city of possibilities and travelled there from Switzerland. This Gusto Gräser moved in with Graf's friend Schorsch one day, and then didn't leave. He claimed he only ever washed in fresh spring-water, and unfortunately there was no spring in Munich. So he remained unwashed—and stank like a goat, as Graf noted. He was a pure apostle of innocence. "He was a thoroughbred vegetarian, with long, wavy Jesus hair and a full beard and moustache to match. He wore a kind of toga made of sackcloth, held together with wooden pegs." He preached texts by Chinese philosophers, passages from Nietzsche's *Zarathustra*, and his own aphorisms, which he wrote on square slips of paper and carried around in a little leather pouch, sometimes giving them away or selling them.

When Graf went to visit his friend Schorsch in these days he greeted the apostle, who had plunged Schorsch's studio into hopeless chaos, with a hostile stare.

"My friend was getting dressed to go out with me. He buttoned his waistcoat.

'Buttons... that's... ahhh... that's absurd... completely absurd,' murmured the apostle.

'Come on,' said Schorsch, and we left.

'Heavens, man, what kind of vermin have you got living with you?' I asked him on the stairs.

'I can't get rid of him,' was the reply.

'What? Just throw him out!' I cried."

But Schorsch doesn't throw him out. The following evening they go to a meeting where Gusto Gräser is due to give a speech.

And he speaks.

"The hall was quite full. There was no smoking allowed. We smoked. It was already rather noisy in there. At the front sat dewy-eyed girls with Heidi plaits, old maids, Wandervogel members, idealistic oddballs and the like." And Spartacists. And the people.

The event is a debacle. Gräser gives a sermon on the spirit of non-violence. "Enough spirits, we need schnapps!" Graf crows. Someone shouts: "Billy goat!" Gräser makes gestures of benediction. He extols the virtues of nature. "Eating grass and lazing about is absurd!" cries Graf. And someone else shouts: "Down with nature! Hurrah for technology!"

Gräser goes on preaching. The crowd mocks him and laughs and larks around. "We are no longer humans!" Gräser shouts. "No, we're beasts!" yells Graf. A Spartacist takes over the stage. Gives the usual propaganda speech. The audience has a splendid time.

After the event, Gusto Gräser goes back to Schorsch's studio. Schorsch's friends mock him; they are coarse, mean and hurtful. All right, says Graf, seeing as he loves nature so much: "Tomorrow, please go and set up camp in the English Garden."

Two days later he really does leave. By day he is still to be seen wandering the streets of Munich, usually followed by a horde of bellowing children. People say he is staying in a goat stall.

But Gusto Gräser is on his way to becoming a kind of global superstar. He just doesn't know it yet. And not under his own name, Gusto Gräser, but in a literary disguise, as someone who leads people on the path inwards, to a new God, to themselves. The name under which he will become famous is "Demian". A story with this title has just been published by S. Fischer Verlag, excerpted in their *Neue Rundschau* magazine before it comes out in book form. The first part in February, the second in the April issue. The story has been written by one Emil Sinclair, a complete unknown. Neither the publisher Samuel Fischer nor the editor Oskar Loerke know who the young debutant is. This Emil Sinclair writes the story of his transformation, as he emerges from the disorientation of the old pre-war period into a new life, a new light. He follows a peculiar friend and leader, eventually forming an alliance with this man and his mother. The peculiar friend, Max Demian, is a wise, innocent preacher. "For a hundred or more years," he explains to his astonished friend Sinclair, "all Europe has done is study and build factories! They know exactly how many grams of powder it takes to kill a man, but they don't know how to pray to God, they don't even know how to be happy for a whole hour."

Max Demian's speeches to his yearning listener go on in a similar vein. "What nature wants of man is written in a few individuals, in you, in me. It was written in Christ, it was written in Nietzsche. For these important currents alone—which can of course assume a different form every day—will there be a place when the communities of today collapse."

Max Demian predicts the coming war, the intoxication that will bind people together. "Perhaps it will be a great war, a very great war. The new world is beginning, and the new world will be terrible for those who cling to the old."

Something new, something never before seen is struggling free on the battlefields of Europe, so this wondrous prophet believes. "A giant bird was struggling out of the egg; the egg was the world and the world must first be rent asunder." Before it can become new, fully and completely new. "Deep down underneath something was taking shape. Something akin to a new humanity."

The book will become a fantastic success in Germany and Europe, and the author will be celebrated as the leading light of Germany's young generation. Thomas Mann is delighted by the story when he reads it a few weeks later. He wonders, just as everyone else is wondering, who this Emil Sinclair could be, and realizes to his surprise that the book is a kind of brother to the *Magic Mountain*, which he has begun to work on again. Here, too, the Great War breaks out "as a solution" at the end of the narrative.

That year, Emil Sinclair will go on to win the Fontane Prize for the best German debut novel. And a year later, he will have to give it back. For this is no debutant—and his name isn't Sinclair, either. The book's author is Hermann Hesse, by then forty-one years old and already famous in the literary world for books like *Beneath the Wheel* and *Peter Camenzind*.

He had met Gusto Gräser early on. In 1907 he had followed this wanderer to Monte Verità in Ticino. Staying in a wooden hut, he spent several weeks with his friend, and for a while Hesse himself lived as a hermit in the cliffs near Gräser's cave at Arcegno, naked, fasting and meditating.

But then Hesse returned to his bourgeois life and was soon mocking Gräser in his spiteful story "Dr Knölge's End", picturing him as a gorilla hanging in the trees.

During the war, the two were reconciled. Hesse became
Gräser's "poetic herald". His reform settlement on Monte
Verità became a "dream island of fulfilment" for Hesse, a
model for "another way of living".

But when the war was over, the egg had been rent asunder,
and Munich, more than anywhere else, seemed to be making
itself ready for a new humanity, the two men went their
separate ways. At the start of 1919 Gusto Gräser wrote to
Hermann Hesse in Bern: "The TREE of life germinates and
grows only of its own accord.—It puts out roots and shoots
when the blocks of ice that make up the economy of objects
and logic no longer hem it in.—Let a warm wind blow into
the land of winter! Let the THAW melt the ice in the frozen
minds of this frozen world." He was on his way to the new
warmth, the beautiful new community and humanity that
he hoped to find in Munich for himself and his fellow man.

And he probably hoped, perhaps he was even sure, that
his friend would follow him to Germany, to Munich. Many
in Germany thought he would. Hermann Hesse, the Swabian
pacifist in Switzerland—where else would he go but Munich?

They were all wrong. Hesse has sent his Demian to
Germany, but he himself is fleeing in the opposite direction.
Many people, or so he writes in his letters, have offered him
political positions in Germany. Join us, Hermann Hesse!
But Hesse doesn't want to. He wants to be free. He has just
left his wife and child. He wants to get back "to the three
consolations of my youth: literary work, alcohol and, in the
background, the comforting thought of suicide". Oh yes, in his
mind he's a radical: "I would be ready to join the Spartacists,
were it not for my moral reservations. Although I believe
suicide is permitted for desperate men, I do not believe in
killing others."

He moves away to his own south. To Ticino. It's the Hesse Revolution. The path into solitude. Far away from everyone. "When I see this blessed place at the southern foot of the Alps again, I feel as if I were returning home from exile, as if I were finally on the right side of the mountains." Here, everything is "neither new nor old, and looks as though it has not been taken from nature by work and trickery, but has been created like rock, tree and moss".

He can only function in solitude, Hesse tells the friends who write urging him to join the worldly revolution. "I cannot convince anyone, I cannot stand my ground verbally against anyone, I cease to be a character, a person of any value, when I sit on the surface of things and am subject to the constant direct influence of people and movements."

Hermann Hesse had sent another text to Germany at the start of the year, in which he put forward his literary, lonely world politics much more directly and combatively than in Demian. It is called *Zarathustra's Return*, and it wasn't published under Hesse's name, either. The essay appeared anonymously. In it, Hesse calls on people to reflect and let things take their course. He fears that these new revolutions will bring new violence, and new ideas for improving the world will only bring new troubles, new suffering. "And that is why you are clamouring for more action, rushing into the streets storming and shouting, electing councils, and loading your guns again. All because you are forever in flight from suffering! In flight from yourselves, from your souls!"

So Hermann Hesse is also preaching in these days. He preaches from his pulpit of solitude, railing against those very people who believe they are making the world a better place. "The world wasn't made to be bettered," he writes in his Zarathustra essay. "Nor were you made to be bettered.

You were made to be yourselves. You were made to enrich the world with a sound, a tone, a shadow. Be yourself, then the world will be rich and beautiful!"

He is writing about himself. About a person who, for a moment, has found himself. "If ever the world has been bettered, if it has ever been made richer, more alive, happier, more dangerous, more amusing, this has not been the work of reformers, of betterers, but of true self-seekers, among whom I should so like to count you. Those earnestly and truly self-seeking men who have no goal and no purposes, who are content to live and to be themselves."

His peculiar long-haired friend with the sandals and the aphorisms in a little leather bag, whose life and speeches had been an example to Hesse in so many ways, has a different plan. He is making speeches, gathering people around him, allowing the nay-sayers to mock him in the city of dreamers and world-betterers. In their own way, both men are trying to bring love into the world.

In his review of a volume of correspondence between Eduard Mörike and Theodor Storm written in these weeks, Hermann Hesse once again describes precisely what the task of authors and literature is—in the spring of 1919 and, in fact, always: "The only thing we can learn from authors", he writes, "is love. To love the world and life, to love even in torment, to welcome every sunbeam with gratitude, and even in our suffering, not to forget entirely how to smile. This lesson from all true literature never grows old, and today it is more necessary and deserving of our gratitude than ever."

The writers down in Munich currently have other things to worry about. How do they hold on to this great opportunity that has been given to them? How do they live up to all the

expectations placed on them? How do they resist the chal-
lenges from all sides? Ernst Toller, the new king of Bavaria,
has had the sceptre of power pressed into his hand and is now
waving it like a magic wand. But it doesn't cast any spells.
Nothing happens by itself. No one is grateful. No one is satisfied, even for a moment. No one gives these inexperienced
poet-politicians any time to get their bearings inside the palace
of power. Time to try things out. Time to convince people.

It's only two days since power fell into Toller's hands, but
already he knows: "This Council Republic was a mistake."

They won't be able to hold on to it. Nothing good will come
of it. It won't end well. It can't end well. They are beset from
left and right, the Freikorps are massing in northern Bavaria,
the left-wing groups are at war with each other in Munich,
and he is besieged by all the people who believe in him, with
their hopes that he can't fulfil. The whole thing is a nightmare.

The new world—a minute ago it was still a splendid sheet
of white paper, on which we could all freely write, paint, plan,
draw our designs. It has very quickly been covered with scrawls
of hate and panic, accusations, mockery, violence.

On the evening of 9th April, a section leader bursts into
Toller's office. Distraught, he explains to the head of government that Toller is to be ousted by the communists that very
evening in the Mathäserkeller. What is going on? Two days
ago the communists declared that Bavaria wasn't ready for a
council republic, and have thus been refusing to participate
and causing chaos—and now they're going to oust us? Why?

Ernst Toller goes over to the beer hall he knows so well.
Eugen Leviné has the floor. He is pouring scorn on the pseudo-
council republic again, the government's incompetence, their
laxity, their weakness. Toller asks to speak. He is refused. He
speaks anyway, his beautiful, emotional rhetoric mixed with

disbelief and anger. If you're prepared to participate now, then the palace is just across the way. Come and join us! You're most welcome. Let us try and work together.

He warns them against toppling the current government: the peasants won't follow a government led by communists alone, and the food-supply situation in the city would become catastrophic within a very short space of time.

That isn't a problem, Leviné retorts, they will do what they did in Russia and force the peasants to provide corn and milk by sending troops out to punish those who refuse. Toller says that didn't even work in Russia, and are they really going to go out to the villages and do battle over every litre of milk?

Leviné doesn't care. The meeting is electing a new government. There are Social Democrats present, too—another thing that was taboo two days ago. An emissary is sent to the Wittelsbach palace to inform the other members of the government that they have been deposed and tell them to stop governing now, please. The newly nominated government leaves the room.

Toller has to stay. Toller is under arrest.

"Couriers come and go, committees are organized, proclamations are drawn up and sealed—they have brought with them the seal of the new council for this eventuality. The tables are still occupied, and sleepy waiters serve beer and sausages. Slowly, the noise of conversation dies down, gestures grow tired, the smoky air hangs heavy over our heads," he writes later.

Then, at two in the morning, there is movement in the cellar. The Council Republic's troops rush in. "We've come to release you!" they shout. The half-asleep crowd doesn't know whether the troops have come to attack them or Toller.

Chaos erupts. "Hands up! Leave the building at once!" shouts the leader. "After three drum rolls, we'll shoot!"

They are already beating the first drum roll. A few people jump out of the windows. Most stay where they are. "Shoot, if you have the courage!" they cry.

Toller is beside himself. "Have you gone mad? Cancel that order at once!" he barks at the leader. He refuses. "Then I will," says Toller, and addresses the soldiers. The leader points a gun at his head, but that's all he does. The troops withdraw.

Who is the government now? Who is the leader? Who is fighting whom? Who is listening to Toller? And who to Leviné? Ernst Toller hurries off to see the City Commandant, where he learns that the communists have urged the workers to storm the barracks and disarm the soldiers. The barracks are on alert. Toller fears a bloodbath.

At six in the morning he leaves the City Commandant's office, dejected, fearful. He sees the trams running: they have not heeded the communists' call to strike. A glimmer of hope. Toller goes into the factories, to Maffei, to Krupp, has them convene general meetings, speaks to the workers in reassuring tones. They reject the idea of marching on the barracks. In the other factories, too, workers decide not to follow the communists.

Split-second governments, pseudo-governments, sudden parallel governments. In these days power floats through the city, unmoored. Someone seizes it; another lets it slip through his fingers. Many grasp at thin air. Many laugh. Revel. Drink. Hope. Fear. To each his own council republic, like that party of merrymakers in the artists' villa in Nymphenburg.

A city wavers between euphoria over a new beginning no one had thought possible, and fear of it.

———

The quiet poet on the periphery, who has barely left the house since the start of the year, who has brought his desk out into the middle of the room and decided to change his life, banishing the outside world (with the exception of women) from his life once more—Rainer Maria Rilke—reflects on the fluctuations out there, as always with great sympathy and with the wisdom of one who lives in books and in love.

A few weeks previously, he wrote to Eva Marie, Baroness Hayl zu Herrnsheim: "As far as I am concerned, despite all my worries there still prevails in me a far-reaching confidence that stretches beyond all this urgency—something that I never felt with regard to the war. It is only now that ideals are actually becoming clear, the most human and most captivating ideals, and we must not be deceived by the fact that the masses subscribe to them in their lumbering, clumsy, helpless way; they don't know any better. Nor must we be deceived by the fact that those who do not yet have faith in the legal maturity of these masses are attempting to shore up their interests with outmoded forms of resistance; if the press's constant river of lies, from which the most deceptive will-o'-the wisps are still rising, was not flowing between the parties, then perhaps one could imagine them reaching an understanding.

"The war could be nothing other than an end; it was extreme by its unnatural nature: mankind terminating itself. Existence had to start afresh after that—we are now in that beginning phase, and the future's first condition is that it cannot be easy: how could it be?

"A difficult, difficult beginning. Nothing new for me: ever since I can remember I have felt like a beginner."

These are the words the poet writes in the centre of his room. But all he does is watch; he watches and sympathizes with the other beginners down there on the street.

Especially him, that curly-haired young man at the head of what currently seems to be the government. Ernst Toller— who is painfully aware that he, too, is a beginner, the greatest beginner of all. Who knows now that it was wrong to plunge so naively into this great beginning. And who is unable to extricate himself from it. His ability to make such good, convincing speeches that hearts fly out to him when he speaks is almost a curse. People trust and believe in him as soon as they see him, hear him. And now he doesn't dare tell them the truth. Later, he will write: "the politician's greatest crime is silence. He must speak the truth, however burdensome it may be; the truth alone can bolster strength, will and reason."

But Toller stays silent and struggles and defends himself and the Council Republic. He has no time left to govern, to use the opportunities for which he came into this and which now lie before him, more freely available than they ever have been.

The only people in the government making a purposeful effort to realize their ideas are Silvio Gesell and Gustav Landauer. These two men, whose first act was to inform their colleagues that from then on, they wanted to be spared paperwork, petty misgivings, bureaucratic nonsense and day-to-day trivialities, are taking great strides with their projects. The one with revolutionizing schools and universities; the other with the introduction of decaying money. They write telegrams, give speeches and draft decrees, curricula and instructions to the banks and universities. "A few weeks" was what Landauer had wished for. He suspects it might be less. He suspects that the dream might remain a dream.

And then, of course, there is Erich Mühsam. The man who was not appointed to a government office, but who has been asked to maintain contact with the governments in Hungary and Russia, and has fought like a berserker on the street and in the palace: writing, versifying, making speeches for the common cause.

He is the first to admit in public and to the communists that it was a mistake to proclaim the Council Republic without them. Meekly, he asks the KPD's Eugen Leviné to work with them all the same. In the style of an official news service, Mühsam reports: "Comrade Leviné assured me that he had absolutely no doubt about the sincerity of my actions. However, he sternly rejected my requests that the KPD become actively involved in the Council Republic. He said that he was personally convinced of the hopelessness of the government's work. When I said, 'But we can't just leave the cart stuck in the mud!' he laconically replied, 'Then pull it out.'"

Mühsam weighs up the result of this diplomatic conversation between differently minded left-wingers: "Although we had not found common ground, we parted with a handshake that transcended personal differences and gave me hope that a political agreement was possible."

In his desperation, Erich Mühsam also turns to Comrade Lenin in Moscow. He tells him of the monstrous difficulties involved in governing this state, and the Bavarian KPD, who are working "with high pressure against us". And he complains: "The task of representing and implementing the necessary revolutionary decisions has rested almost entirely on my shoulders."

He paints himself as a friend to communism, in the hope of prompting Lenin to exercise his authority over the Bavarian KPD. But Lenin takes his time. He doesn't reply until 27th April, when he sends a wireless message to Munich: "We thank you for your greeting and welcome wholeheartedly the Soviet Republic in Bavaria. We would also ask you to provide us with frequent, detailed reports on the measures you have taken in the struggle against the bourgeois hangmen Scheidemann et al." There follow numerous revolutionary tips, desires, demands. Signed off with a friendly: "Best wishes for your success. Lenin." The telegram will not reach the Council Republic.

But in these early days of April, Erich Mühsam is at the height of his labours. The perfect victim for the jocular reporter Ben Hecht from Chicago, who is, as ever, prone to exaggeration and on the lookout for scurrilous material on the operatic Bavarian Revolution to send home to his eager readers. To his mind:

The oddest of the lot was Mühsam. Dictator Toller was worried about him.

"We have been discussing whether we should arrest him," said Toller, "for his own good. I decided against it—for the time being."

Mühsam was in disfavour because of the trouble he created in the streets. He had commandeered a small motor lorry for his personal use. In this he toured the Munich streets. Whenever he saw a crowd, he stopped his lorry, stood up on its seat and started an address. He usually began with a recitation of his famous revolutionary poem, "The Sun of Liberty".

Thousands of workers were still idling in the streets as if a picnic and not a revolution were going on. They took an aversion to their lyrical spokesman, Erich Mühsam. As soon as he started reciting his poetry, they would start yelling and waving their guns. Several times they had stormed his lorry and pulled him off his stage. Once shooting had started and he had had to run for his life."

It wasn't quite like that. There was no poem by Mühsam called "The Sun of Liberty", either. But Mühsam did have something of the holy fool about him. He was driven by a belief in the good in people, the power of literature, the ideals of anarchism. And Ben Hecht was right when he cabled to Chicago: "Mühsam's troubles could not touch his happiness. The people were free. The sun of liberty was shining on them. Justice had come into the world. Mühsam walked in utopia and his heart overflowed."

The image of him reciting his poems, always and everywhere, was also correct. And he was constantly writing new poems. He had just composed his "Council Marseillaise"— which, of course, had to be brought to the ears of people on the street at once. Why else had he written it?

> Oh nations, how long will you tarry?
> The day is dawning; night is gone.
> Will you forever dream of freedom
> While freedom rises like the sun?
> Hear the calls from out the east!
> Unite, unite, in word and deed!
> Liberation is at hand!
> Let your resolve burn like a brand!
> Oh nations, up and join the fight!
> Give the brothers now your word.
> Freedom is the battle-cry,
> And the councils are the sword.

Then comes the night before Palm Sunday. In the early evening, Ernst Toller receives a phone call from someone who refuses to give his name. All he says is: "I want to warn you that there is a putsch being planned against the council government."

Toller wavers. After all, there is always some kind of putsch being planned. On the other hand: he knows that the first troops raised by Johannes Hoffmann's exile government in Bamberg are at the gates of Munich. And he suspects that in a successful putsch, the Bamberg troops wouldn't just arrest him briefly and then let him go. This vague premonition makes Toller take the caller's warning seriously. He spends the night of 12th April at a friend's house.

No one has warned Erich Mühsam. Or the other people's delegates. At around four o'clock in the morning, Mühsam is dragged out of bed by the so-called Republican Protection Force, which just a short time ago swore unconditional loyalty to the council government. They arrest him and take him to the railway station.

It has really happened. Some of the republican troops have switched sides; people are saying that the Bamberg government has promised them 300 marks each. They have forced their way into the Wittelsbach palace, arrested the people's delegates still working there, and snatched others, like Mühsam, from their beds. Thirteen members of the Central Council, including Silvio Gesell and the eager Housing Commissioner Wadler, are taken to the main station, which the putschists have also seized in order to maintain their connection to the exile government in Bamberg and other counter-revolutionaries within the state.

Before dawn, posters are put up around the station declaring that the Central Council has been deposed, and proclaiming Hoffmann's government. The posters are signed: "Munich Garrison". The commander of the troops at the railway station is the Social Democrat Aschenbrenner. By morning, the putschists' soldiers are patrolling the city. The Munich branch of the SPD stands firmly behind them.

The dream is over. Less than a week after the writers took power, reality has won back control over palace and station and streets. That's what it looks like.

The city, the citizens, are completely confused. The city reels. Who is governing? Who is fighting whom? What next? Is this all some kind of joke? Or the reverse: is it the end of all jokes for evermore? Rumours are all people have to go on. There are no reliable newspapers, just posters and leaflets and whispers.

The arch-conservative Josef Hofmiller, who wanted to get rid of Kurt Eisner by carrying him off into the mountains, has also heard about that morning's developments. He notes: "Posters have been put up 'from the whole Munich garrison', saying that they back Hoffmann's government. Very nice, coming from these costumed ruffians, who just a week ago were still declining to protect the government and the Landtag with a great show of emotion; at that point they were backing the council government. Has the Bamberg government increased their wages by fifty pfennigs a day?"

Even people who oppose the councils aren't taking their opponents' opponents entirely seriously. Though in the villa on the Herzogpark Thomas Mann, who has now begun work on *The Magic Mountain* again, harbours a growing hatred. Hatred for those who are turning fictions into reality. He is fighting for the fictionality of fiction, for the true freedom of art. On this Palm Sunday, 13th April, Thomas Mann writes his final word on the writers' republic in his diary: "For the time being I welcome the overthrow of the soviet government. Everywhere there are people who believe that it will come back, that 'it' is inevitable, and to a large extent I share that belief. But there is a great difference between theory and practice, and I loathe irresponsible 'revolutionaries' who are a disgrace to intellectual life, like the lads who have ruined it for this time. I would have no objection if they were shot [...], but we had best be careful not to."

Wait it out. Munich is still a stage. A stage on which Ernst Toller has taken refuge in a friend's apartment. When he wakes, the telephone is ringing. The friend answers and repeats loudly everything the caller is telling him so that Toller can listen in: "Putsch against the Council Republic succeeding... Hoffmann's troops have taken the station... all the members of the Central Council arrested... Mühsam, Hagemeister... Wadler... only Toller and Leviné still at large, but we're already hot on their trail."

Time is tight, then. The doorbell rings. The friend hides Toller in a small cubbyhole behind the bookcase. They are out of luck: it's a lieutenant from the army. They're in luck: he's looking for a woman, not socialists. He has just returned from Turkey and he wants nothing more to do with the monarchy since hearing that Kaiser Wilhelm has fled to Holland. Ah, good.

Toller comes out of his hiding place and asks the lieutenant if he can borrow his uniform so that he can go safely out onto the street without being arrested. The lieutenant beams: "With pleasure... I'll give it to you along with all the orders and ribbons. I just want one thing in return. When you get back into power you must give me an aeroplane so that I can fly to the North Pole and marry an Eskimo girl and forget this whole bloody continent."

Very well, it's a deal.

Toller pulls on the uniform, transforms himself into a putschist, goes into the street, is saluted by other soldiers, salutes them back and sets off for the station. What must the place look like by now?

There is a battle in progress. Workers and some members of the protection force aren't going to let a few hundred turncoats take their new republic away from them just like that. To the station! the cry echoes through the streets. And the workers begin to mass.

Oskar Maria Graf and his friends from Nymphenburg are running towards the station, too. From some distance away they can hear shots, the thunder of cannon, the rattle of machine guns. What is going on? Who is fighting whom? "Putsch! Barricades!" Chief Censor Achenbach wheezes at them. There are planes overhead. Flyers rain down. People start to tussle over the flyers. "Central Council deposed!" they say. "Foreign agitators who are just pursuing their own interests!" they say. Soldiers aim their rifles into the air and fire at the planes, there is a deafening racket, hatred, shouting. "Scheppenhorst lies!" "Majority Socialist traitors!"

More and more people are gathering, more armed men rushing towards the station. "Down! Down! Down!" they shout. The rat-a-tat of machine guns. Graf sees the communist Josef Sontheimer run past him, two machine guns hanging from his shoulders. "Forward! On! Attack!" he bellows. Everyone dashes after him; people who have been shot fall down, detonations shake the ground and the buildings, and the crowd in which Graf finds himself pushes onward into the uproar of the station.

A wild, angry crowd. It all seems to happen automatically. A feeling has taken on a life of its own. It pulls everyone along.

Graf writes:

No gun! I'm simply going to get shot to bits like a lump of flesh, was the thought whirring round my addled head, and with clenched teeth, with clenched fists I was driven onward by the crowd. All at once I shouted in the ears of the people jammed against me: "Good God, what is going on here! Whom are we actually fighting?" The anger in my voice made the bodies pressing around me tremble in fright. I was on the point of grabbing someone and tearing him to pieces in a blind rage, just so I wouldn't be shot down for nothing. And alongside it, the constant thought: stupid! So stupid! Always finding yourself in the middle of a mob and never having a purpose.

That day more or less taught me how a coward can become a hero.

"We're fighting the Bamberg troops! We're fighting Hoffmann, you dolt!" came the reply, and I felt a clear sense of relief. "Well then! That's all right! Let's go! Let's go!" I said. The shooting had died down, and shouts echoed through the high-ceilinged halls: "Victory! Victory! Long live the Council Republic!"

And the victory really is at hand. The workers, the communists, the independents, the proletarians—a disparate angry mob has repelled the attack. Though admittedly too late for Mühsam and the other members of the Central Council, who have been taken north out of the city on a special train with a heavy military escort, to the jail in Ebrach.

Ernst Toller has taken no part in the fighting, either. While it was still going on, the factory councils gathered, believing that the entire Central Council had been arrested, and elected a new government, a new Central Council, this time under communist leadership.

Yes, *now* the communists are ready. Max Levien, Eugen Leviné and the others. They see that what sense and reason could not unite has now been united by the failed counter-revolution. They see, or they want to see, that the proletariat has finally come together. They see that the despised pseudo-council republic is not capable of survival. That it is now time to move from a sham to a real, communist-led council republic. Enough of the "platitude-politics of the boy Toller", as Leviné had intoned several days before. We are engaged in real struggles. We can no longer afford to have romantic, peace-loving aesthetes in charge. Time for us. Time for deeds, not words. Time for the communists.

After the victory at the station, Ernst Toller goes to the City Commandant's office, where the new Council is meeting, to see where the balance of power now lies. Once again he is arrested on sight. "Now we have the king of southern Bavaria," Max Levien jokes. Toller speaks in his own defence, there is some discussion, and eventually he is released again. He is even accepted back into the government. Eugen Leviné's wife Rosa asks her husband what it is about Toller. Leviné replies: "One cannot simply shake off a man who 'wants to die for the proletariat'."

No, Toller isn't going to be shaken off. It's his republic. These are his people, and they believe in him. Whether the Council Republic is real or a sham, he's there to stay. That evening he returns to his guest house exhausted.

The fat housemaid shrieks when she sees him. As if he were a spectre, a dead man come to visit. And in fact: "We thought you were dead," she cries. The guest house has been full of soldiers all day, hoping to catch him. Until it became clear that their comrades at the station had suffered a defeat, and the putsch had been subdued. Then they turned tail and ran, with Toller's collection of ties in their packs. "They didn't leave a single one," the housemaid tells the returning poet.

And now? Will everyone now start working together? The "pseudo-republicans" who are still at liberty release official declarations. Toller announces: "Workers! Your achievements are under threat! Protect the revolution with your bodies, your will and your hearts! Long live the Bavarian Council Republic! Long live the World Revolution! Munich, the 14th of April 1919, Ernst Toller." Ernst Niekisch diplomatically pledges "to recognize the existing fifteen-member committee as the current legal Central Council". And Gustav Landauer, who only escaped arrest because he had changed hotels the previous night, declares: "The energetic intervention of the proletariat in Munich has saved the Council Republic from the brazen attempted putsch by the counter-revolution. I recognize and welcome the attendant reorganization. The old Central Council no longer exists; I offer my strength, wherever I may be needed, to the campaign committee. Gustav Landauer."

"Wherever I may be needed." Landauer already knew no one needed him any longer. He was an anti-communist. He hated Leviné and his dogmatism, his severity and his readiness for violence. And Leviné and the communists despised Landauer and treated him as an opponent. Against all reason, however, Landauer still hoped to be called upon. Hoped that the wind would change again and surprise them all. He'd had mere moments to realize his plans. Six short days. Despite all his determination—"Here comes Landauer!"—despite all his haste, and even though the plans had been ready beforehand, in his head, in his books. It hadn't been long enough. They simply *had* to call on him and let him continue his work. He moved in with Kurt Eisner's widow, into what had been their marital apartment. And waited.

Two days later, on 16th April, it is clear to him once and for all that he can stop waiting. The new Council Republic is not his republic any more. They aren't going to call on him. And he is no longer willing, either. He writes them a farewell letter.

I have continued to offer my services to the Council Republic in the matter of liberation and the beautiful life... You have so far not taken up my offer. I have now seen you at work and have become familiar with your methods of public instruction, your way of leading the struggle. I have seen what your reality looks like, in contrast to what you call the "pseudo-republic". I have a rather different understanding of the struggle to create a set of circumstances that will allow everyone to share in what the earth and culture provide. When socialism is realized, it immediately enlivens all creative powers: but in your works I see—and lament at seeing—that you have no skill in economic and intellectual areas. Far be it from me to disrupt in the slightest the difficult work of defence that you are carrying out. But I lament bitterly that only a tiny fragment of my work, the work of warmth and recovery, of culture and rebirth, is now being done.

Yes, the work of warmth is over. The new focus is severity and defence and struggle. Twenty men lost their lives in the battle at the main station. The government is now working flat out to form a Red Army. Once again, posters go up asking citizens to hand in their weapons. But this time they are offered an additional incentive: "Anyone who does not surrender his gun within twelve hours will be shot."

The new government takes great pains to show its opponents and the general population that they are no longer being ruled by humanitarian dreamers. This government is made up of professional revolutionaries, many of them from Russia—well trained, resolute, experienced, hard.

But it is not only the new government that has transformed the atmosphere in the city into a cocktail of panic and determination, the readiness to fight and the desire to flee, within a very short space of time. A noose is also gradually tightening around the city. How many counter-revolutionaries are out there? No one knows for certain, of course. On the day of the station putsch, the Hoffmann government announced it would now request armed assistance from Berlin. Gustav Noske, the first Social Democratic Defence Minister, had been waiting for this moment, and agreed at once. Twenty thousand men are on their way from Berlin, with perhaps 22,000 soldiers from the Freikorps and the regular army on top of that, and 3,700 men who have come over from Württemberg. Munich's Red Army numbers 15,000 at most.

In addition to this, food supplies are getting low. The peasants are hardly providing anything now, and the besiegers prevent the little they do supply from getting through whenever they can. The new government starts to confiscate food from hotels and restaurants. A call goes out for a general strike. The publication of all newspapers is banned. Finally the postal, telegraph and telephone services are completely shut down as well. Munich is cut off from the world. All the air has gone out of the city of dreamers.

Ernst Toller flounders in a net of consequences woven by his early enthusiasm: "I should have considered in advance the possibility that bloodshed would follow and not taken up office.

Anyone who wants to fight today on a political level, bringing together economic and human interests, must know that the law and consequences of his struggle will be determined by forces other than his own good intentions; that some form of defence and counter-defence will often be forced upon him, and he will experience these as a tragedy that may, in the most profound sense of the words, bleed him dry."

It is the evening of 15th April. Eugen Leviné is giving a speech to the factory councils and Toller is listening, when suddenly the city begins to quake with the noise of alarm bells. Not a gentle, inviting peal, but alarm bells: loud, fast, tolling continuously. What does this mean? Who gave the order to ring them?

Toller rushes off, accompanied by seven workers. Where is the ringing coming from? Strange: he knows the city, knows the churches and their bells, but this noise seems to be coming from everywhere.

Keeping their heads down, they run along Theatinerstraße. Are the Freikorps already in the city? The ringing has stopped. The silence is almost more eerie. They press on, warily, through the largely deserted streets to the cathedral, the Frauenkirche. They drag the sexton out of bed. He trembles, and his wife begs them not to kill him. Toller reassures her: no one wants to shoot sextons here, he would just like to know if he rang the bells, and why.

No, he didn't. It might have been St Paul's.

So Toller's troop creeps across the deserted Marienplatz to the station, where the Reds are encamped. They confirm it: yes, it was St Paul's, it's occupied. There is an abandoned machine gun standing by a pillar; they take it with them and head for St Paul's.

Fifty paces from the church they set up the gun, and one of the men fires it at the church tower. A window opens, and someone shouts indignantly: "Oh, very nice, this is: they're even shooting in the middle of the night now."

The little troop races over to the church that is said to be under enemy occupation. Everything is quiet. They politely ring the verger's doorbell—Where are the Whites? "None here." Who gave him the order to ring the bells? "How should I know?" Ah, so he *is* in league with the Whites—that much is clear! "What do you mean, Whites? How'm I supposed to recognize every last flaming Spartacist? The order came from the Sendling section."

And so, on to Sendling. There, in the communists' local base, they are told that the order came from the City Commandant's office. The Freikorps are apparently on their way to Munich. Those were warning bells.

Where are the Freikorps now? No one knows.

Toller and his troop press on towards Allach. At an inn on the Nymphenburg road they meet three soldiers from the cavalry regiment. They've had enough of fighting; they grumble about the beer and gladly give their horses to Toller and his men for their journey.

Finally, near Karlsfeld, Toller meets a group of workers and soldiers who have joined forces on the spur of the moment and beaten back the troops who were trying to tighten the ring around Munich.

Now the enemy is out of sight, and the group is starting to fall apart. They need someone to keep them together and drive them forward, someone with a strategy to force the counter-revolutionaries back towards Dachau. They say Toller should do it. Toller laughs. He should do what? Take charge of a battery? No, of the whole corps, this newly formed section of the Red Army.

Good joke. Toller is a pacifist who wrote a play about his

transformation, and he's never led a military unit. And now, in the middle of the night, they expect him to take charge of Bavaria's Red Army? Why?

"Someone's got to show some backbone, or this'll be a shambles—and if you don't know how, you'll learn. Main thing is, we know you, see."

Fine. Toller is moved. Toller will do it.

He rides back to Munich; he needs maps. There are none left in the War Ministry. Toller suspects that reactionary officers took them away with them just in case.

Rudolf Egelhofer, the new City Commandant and Commander-in-Chief of the Red Army, orders his new general to bombard Dachau with artillery and then storm it. No negotiations.

Toller goes back to the front. He hesitates. Dachau's peasants are on his side—he knows that. He issues an ultimatum to the counter-revolutionaries: withdraw your troops to the other side of the Donau, release the imprisoned members of the Central Council and end the blockade on supplies to Munich. Negotiators are sent back and forth. Finally they are told that the Bamberg government has relented and is prepared to accept the conditions, though they will only withdraw as far as Pfaffenhofen.

Then suddenly, the sound of gunfire. Have the Bamberg troops broken the ceasefire already? No, the shots came from their own side. Who gave the order?

Attacking while negotiations are still going on? Have all the rules been abandoned in this war? This is madness. Toller decides to go to Dachau himself to clear up the incident.

Halfway there, the gunfire starts again. And once more, it's their own troops pushing forward. What is Toller supposed to do? He lets the advance continue. He himself retreats to Karlsfeld to mobilize reserves and lead them back to Dachau.

Many of the workers from Dachau are on the attackers' side. The men and women from the Dachau munitions factory join them at once. "The women among them were even more determined than the men," writes Toller. They disarm the exile government's troops and drive them out of the town. The commandant of the Bamberg troops escapes in a locomotive. The battle is won.

The pacifist poet and playwright is astonished. "Me? I am the victor of Dachau?" But he hasn't done anything. He just went with the flow. Was carried along by events, by the workers' front.

They have taken prisoners, including officers of the counter-revolution. City Commandant Egelhofer sends a telegram from Munich at once. The officers are to be summarily court-martialled and shot. Toller tears up the order as soon as he receives it. He wants the officers to see that the communists are humane and fraternal. They need to see for themselves that all the rumours spreading across the state about brutal, unscrupulous, murdering communists are untrue. That they are brothers.

Toller lets the officers go. A few days later they will be back fighting the Reds.

But Toller refuses to be deterred: "However brutal the rules of civil war may be, I know that in Berlin the counter-revolutionaries murdered Red prisoners in cold blood, and we are fighting for a better world; we are calling for humanity and must show humanity ourselves."

He wants to do everything differently. And he wants to begin at once. Now that he is the victor of Dachau, this is surely a good time for it. If not now, then when?

"The imperial army was run by authority and blind obedience; the Red Army is to be founded on free will and understanding. We must not copy the old, detested militarism. The Red soldier will not be treated like a machine; he knows that he is fighting for his own cause, and discipline will result from his individual revolutionary will."

But this is a battle Ernst Toller cannot win. The battle against the German spirit of subservience. The battle against the might of military reality.

He knows it himself: "Alas, the German workers have been accustomed to blind obedience for too long, and want only to obey. They confuse brutality with strength, bluster with leadership, the removal of individual responsibility with discipline. They miss their old ideals and believe that chaos is breaking out."

The rulers in Munich fly into a rage when they hear of Toller's disobedience. What kind of general disregards orders from the army's supreme command? Where will this soft-heartedness lead? Over the days that follow, there are numerous heated disputes between Leviné and Toller in Munich. Leviné is utterly baffled by Toller's naivety, his eagerness to debate, willingness to contradict and deafness to instructions. Toller says he just acts as the situation and his heart instruct him. Anyway, he says, he is now being called back into the field. He has no time for this infighting. His soldiers are waiting.

Out near Dachau, his door is flung open one evening. Some men bring in a distraught young girl on a stretcher, fearful, gasping for breath, her clothes torn. They found her in the soldiers' sleeping quarters. "More than twenty of the Red Guard have taken a turn with her," one of them explains. Toller orders them to take the girl to the field hospital; he goes with them. On the way, the men tell him what has happened. It is the story of something unleashed in war, of men in a frenzy, here on this small front line for which Ernst Toller is responsible.

He thinks back to the Great War, from which he somehow escaped alive. The horror. The "never again!" of that time. He sees the girl; he looks closely. Later he will write: "Here I see the war, naked and brutal, Wilhelm II once called war a 'bath of steel'. The German professors claim that it rouses the nation's moral and ethical conscience. Just as you like, gentlemen, but don't tell me that this story proves the depravity of the Reds. Your own heroes, if they are honest, could cite a thousand such episodes from the 'Great' War."

On the way to the field hospital, Toller encounters another girl in a similar state to the one they are already taking to the doctors. Chaos reigns, raw exhilaration and fear. A moment ago he was the hero of Dachau, but now Ernst Toller is trapped in the middle of a civil war, powerless to control the mayhem. Around 1,000 of the 2,000-strong troop that captured Dachau have decided to take an impromptu holiday and set off towards Munich. The remaining men are still drinking to the victory and refuse to stop. Toller bans the nearby inns from serving alcohol.

And then new, nonsensical orders arrive from the city. Withdraw the troops from Dachau: they want to form a ring around Munich.

The telegrams from Munich remind Toller of the confused messages sent by the mad Foreign Minister, Dr Lipp. He hurries back into the city and asks Leviné to explain these ridiculous plans to him; he appeals to the factory councils, who are still loyal to him. Then he heads back out to his troops, towards the final defeats. It isn't far to go now.

COUNTER-SHOT

IT IS EASTER SUNDAY, a mild, blue spring day. The 20th of April, a week after the Palm Sunday putsch at the station. There is a tense silence in the city. Will communism really last? And if so, which communism? Toller's? Leviné's? The communism of Thomas Mann, which he, going joyfully out into the street, would happily celebrate for its enmity towards the Entente? The earthy, peasant communism of Oskar Maria Graf? Or will the counter-revolution win? Their circle around Munich is gradually closing in. Will they take and liberate the city? Liberate it in what sense? Where will they take it? Into what kind of freedom? Into what new order?

A city between worlds.

On Ludwigstraße and Schellingstraße, the streets are black with people, the pavements crowded with men, women and children coming out of Mass. A military vehicle decked with red pennants speeds past and the crowd parts in fear. Young men in threadbare uniforms, rifles shouldered, squat on the truck bed, shouting and whooping. Hunting people, just for fun. The young reporter from Leipzig, Victor Klemperer, watches the scene. It's a familiar sight: "Not a single day goes by that this reckless driving, which is just a lark, does not claim victims. This is how one dies for freedom!"

A strange mixture of light-heartedness and panic every-where. Springtime, the mood optimistic and apocalyptic at once. It tears the city to shreds—and people go out strolling. The starving and the adventurous hunt pheasants in the English Garden. In this explosive mood, anything can happen there, too. Klemperer writes: "But whenever Mair Franz shoots pheasants in the English Garden, Xaver Huber on Feilitzschplatz thinks the Whites are staging a coup, so he shoots, too, and then the guard at the nearby Church of the Redeemer rings the alarm bell, and soon there's the clatter of gunfire for a quarter of an hour all around. This is very amusing." He knows a small boy, Klemperer writes, whose first words are "rat-a-tat", having listened to the constant machine-gun fire on the streets.

It is comical and terrible at once. What is this doing to Munich's children, who register and remember these sounds more clearly than anything else in their young lives?

Klaus Mann, a bookish, precocious child in early adolescence, who chose Eisner to be the tragic hero of his early play, later reflected on and wrote about this at great length. About the shattering effect that growing up in Munich at that time had on him and his generation. It didn't matter whether you had any interest in it, whether it touched your soul. There was no choice. It touched everyone: "All the same, I caution against underestimating the influence that these political events must have had on a receptive boy, who in the year 1919 was twelve and thirteen years old. He was utterly clueless in relation to *what* was occurring: *that* something was occurring, he sensed without question... He sensed it as an animal feels the approach of an earthquake. As he sat at his school desk, he sensed that an economic order and a scale of moral values were about to be thrown to the dogs. The economic order interested him less at the time. But the crisis of European morality was something he was aware of earlier, since it might have been conducive to a 'normal development'."

He was growing up in a city marooned in no-man's-land. A thousand-year-old dynasty had fled the city, an unlosable war had been lost, writers, cloud-people, had taken power, Munich's residents were continually firing guns from their own front doorways, and no one even knew whom they were shooting at. It is clear, Klaus Mann writes later, "that this must necessarily cast a shadow over the notions this boy forms later about the value and persistence of human ideas and sacred virtues. If one is constantly—whether consciously or unconsciously—waiting for the 'catastrophe', then one is driven mad by values that, it would seem, are no longer strong enough to halt the approach of this catastrophe."

Now, at Easter, the young Klaus Mann spends hours kneeling in the vestibule, writing a polemic against religion. He probably likes to be seen writing. Ultimately his text is an outcry. A protest. It begins: "I do not believe. Since I stopped believing in Father Christmas and the stork bringing babies, I no longer believe in religion, either." And he quotes Martin Luther who, contemplating how he recognized God's benevolence, decided that it was: "By how he rules the world." That just makes the twelve-year-old laugh. He writes: "Look at this war! Look at this mass misery! Look at these beasts in the big cities! Look at the strongmen who are triumphing everywhere—and then say: God rules the world with a benevolent hand!"

All around him on this Easter Sunday, the atmosphere is both festive and febrile. The arrival of the Manns' sixth child has been overdue for days. Katia is suffering. The birth could start at any moment. But it doesn't. There was heavy shooting again overnight, and the church bells rang. Another attack? Raids?

The weather is glorious, and the four older Mann children set off for the Aumeister, a beer garden in the English Garden, to eat tomato soup. Katia's mother comes to visit. She says a lady in the city told her with absolute certainty that it would "all be over by Tuesday". There are still no newspapers, no post. They are cut off from the world. "Under the council government there is complete Sunday rest," Thomas Mann notes.

He sits down at his desk. Gets out the good paper to which he has become accustomed since the *Reflections of a Nonpolitical Man*. And starts to write. A story from ancient times, already "quite covered in a patina of historical rust," writes the storyteller who calls himself "the whispering summoner of the imperfect tense". In fact, this tale is not all that old, he writes; its "sense of a bygone age" comes from "the fact that it plays out before a certain change that left a great chasm running through life and consciousness... It plays, or, to avoid the present tense, it played out and had played out earlier, before, in the old days, the world before the Great War, at the start of which so many things began that even now have scarcely stopped beginning."

Thomas Mann had already begun to write this story once—earlier, before, in the old days. But then came the war, and even as it was breaking out he knew he would use it "as a solution" at the end of his narrative. And before he could do that, the war had to end.

Now it is over. Its end was utterly different from the ending it should have had, and now history, and the novel, begins afresh. Thomas Mann underlines the sentence he writes in his diary on this Easter Sunday. He regards it as historic even as he writes it down. "*After an interruption of four years I have begun to work on 'The Magic Mountain' again.*" He writes a new foreword, gives the novel's hero a grandfather to anchor him

197

deep in the imperfect tense of history. In the "great-great-great" of history.

It is the story of Hans Castorp, a pale German hero who travels to the Berghof sanatorium in Davos to visit his consumptive cousin Joachim Ziemßen. The world up there, the sick pre-war world, will take him captive. He will linger up there for seven years—because he is (probably) sick, yes, but above all because he was ready for sickness. Because he is not sufficiently capable of resisting the forces that draw him up into the fairy-tale world of the lovelorn and the bored. Up into the kingdom of the dead, up into the mountains. The engineer Hans Castorp, who forgets his obligations, turns his back on the world of bourgeois efficiency and avoids reading the newspapers until the news is old, this Hans Castorp is the German pre-war dreamer par excellence. The people on the Magic Mountain represent European society, which has been idle for so long and has bedded down so comfortably in a sense of everlasting safety—until finally the boredom, the tedium of the eternal return of the same in an overly predictable world, result in that "great petulance" that ultimately leads straight into the world war.

But Hans Castorp is also a hero born in revolutionary Munich. A hero caught between the opposing forces of his time. Between the enthusiast for democratic progress Lodovico Settembrini, the middle-aged hard-line communist Leo Naphta, and the beautiful Kyrgyz woman Clawdia Chauchat. These are the magnetic fields in which Castorp finds himself. The three forces that do battle for his soul: the West; the East; love. Or perhaps: democracy; communism; anti-politics. Or even: enlightenment; terrorism; decline.

Hans Castorp finds everything "worth listening to". He stumbles from one pole to the next. A hero like his creator, who one day drinks a toast to communism and the next wants to have all communists shot. It will take more than three years of writing and 600 pages for Hans Castorp to renounce the dark forces and realize that loving the abyss, forgetting one's obligations and having sympathy with death, will lead to calamity. Politically and personally. The love of anti-democracy, of German Romanticism remains deeply anchored within Hans Castorp. But during his closest brush with death, when he gets lost in a snowstorm and nearly perishes, he decides to make a lifelong commitment: "I will keep faith with death in my heart, but also remember that faith with death and things past is only malice and dark lust and misanthropy, if we give it power over our thoughts and actions." And there follows the only sentence in the whole book printed in italics: *"For the sake of goodness and love, man should not allow death mastery over his thoughts."*

Now, on this glorious Easter Sunday in Munich, Thomas Mann cannot yet write this sentence. He doesn't yet sense which path his wavering hero will take. Which path he himself, Munich, Bavaria, Germany will take. Anything is possible.

Nineteen years later, Thomas Mann will write about a brother, an artist like himself. An unsuccessful artist who gave himself over entirely to the dark side and went into politics. At the end of this essay, he will write, full of hope: "More clearly and happily than ever will the artist of the future realize his mission as a white enchanter, as a winged, hermetic, moon-sib mediator between spirit and life."

The essay from 1938 in which Thomas Mann writes these sentences bears the title "Bruder Hitler". A year later, it is published in *Esquire* magazine as "That Man is My Brother". It is a confession of an embarrassing relationship. The writer recognizes himself in the man who has ruled Germany as a dictator for five years. There is so much in Hitler that he also sees in himself: "But there is also present the insatiable craving for compensation, the urge to self-glorification, the restless dissatisfaction, the forgetfulness of past achievements, the swift abandonment of the prize once grasped, the emptiness and tedium, the sense of worthlessness as soon as there is nothing to do to take the world's breath away; the sleepless compulsion to make one's mark on *something*."

On Easter Sunday 1919, this brother is celebrating his thirtieth birthday. He celebrates it wearing a red armband. All the soldiers in Munich wear a red armband now. A few days earlier his life changed direction. At the start of April, he was elected to office for the first time in his life. Not a very important office—not yet. But still the most important thing a soldier in his company can be elected for. Adolf Hitler has become the *Vertrauensmann*, the soldiers' representative, for the Second Demobilisation Company. A position in which he must support and uphold the council government. He has the task of ensuring the smooth running of operations in his regiment, and functions as a middle-man between his regiment and the revolutionaries.

We don't know exactly which political movement he favoured. Many later claimed he was a follower of the Majority Social Democrats. Erhard Auer, Kurt Eisner's adversary, said as much in 1923. And Hitler himself was still speaking of Auer with great respect in the 1940s. In any case, at that point he was not openly opposed to the council government; otherwise his comrades, ninety per cent of whom had voted for the left in the Landtag elections, would hardly have elected him as their representative in these politically heated times.

The historian Thomas Weber writes of Adolf Hitler during these days: "The real significance of the winter and spring of 1919, during which Adolf Hitler was a cog in the machine of socialism, does not lie in the political sphere. Rather, it lies in his having brought about, through expediency and opportunism, a sudden radical transformation of his personality. Almost overnight Hitler had changed from being an awkward but well-liked loner in whom no one had seen any leadership qualities to being a leader in the making."

A leader, however, who wisely steered clear of the power struggles in these days. Even on Palm Sunday, when the first council government had been toppled and the exile government's troops were growing desperate, holding out for hours in the hope that Munich's soldiers would come over, tip the balance in their favour and help them to victory, Hitler's company didn't lift a finger for either side. When Leviné's communist council government came into power, the new rulers demanded fresh elections in Munich's military companies, to secure the "unreserved" support of the company representatives. This time the position was called "battalion councillor", and those elected represented their companies in the battalion soldiers' council. Unreserved support? Adolf Hitler put himself up for election again—but this time he came second, receiving nineteen votes while thirty-nine went to the victor. Hitler was duly elected as his unit's deputy battalion councillor.

At the same time, in these days he becomes increasingly isolated. His lifelong friend, his quiet twin Ernst Schmidt, has left the battalion. He has had enough of this ersatz family. The most important person to Hitler leaves him behind. But now he has this position. A first taste of responsibility. He's a little leader for the first time.

With an entirely uncertain future.

The man who much later—and this time seems an incredibly long way off—will become his deputy is also in Munich in these days. Rudolf Heß lives just a few hundred metres from Hitler's barracks. He is twenty-four years old and largely occupied with writing letters to reassure his worried parents about the situation in the council city. After the proclamation of the first council government he had written: "As a Council Republic has now been proclaimed, the majority of Munich is celebrating and going for walks in the fine weather. Otherwise, nothing is happening." And on 23rd April, he informs them: "I have seen nothing of any unrest. Yesterday there was an orderly procession with red flags. In general, life is the same as ever. Last Thursday there was apparently a brief struggle at the station. But I was in the 'Faust' and heard nothing of it."

What a deceptive calm. The ring around the city is slowly tightening. Food is in increasingly short supply. Of course, those who are rich and canny continue to eat like kings, even in these days. Easter Sunday at the Mann house: "Strong-flavoured smoked pork and *Sachertorte*." It isn't true that the blockade is keeping all provisions out of the city. You just need connections. And money. Or a gun.

Toller, for example, who has just come hurrying back from Dachau, writes the following instruction on Easter Sunday: "Brüller, who owns a cake shop, was forced to hand over cakes etc. to soldiers from the Red Army without payment, using up one centner flour and thirty pounds sugar. The municipal authority is therefore instructed to provide his shop with one centner flour and thirty pounds sugar without billing him. Toller."

The Dutchman's drinking villa is, of course, another place where there are no shortages. He holds a great Easter banquet. Pegu writes a song, the Dutchman sits down at the piano and composes a melody for it, he sings, Pegu sings, and finally everyone—Marietta of Monaco, Ado von Achenbach, Oskar Maria Graf—belts out:

> Brothers, we're fighting the good fight for freedom!
> Onward, my brothers and into the fray!
> A victory here is a vict'ry for ever!
> Brothers, unite and we shall win the day!

Graf crows: "This revolution has no song! That's the terrible thing!" They all laugh.

Achenbach cries: "We're winning!"

Graf tells him: "We're losing. But they can't kill the revolution now."

Meanwhile a thin, consumptive poet with large glasses, who once wrote a wonderful little "romantic novel from Schwabing" about Marietta of Monaco, has set off for Bavaria from Switzerland, having heard about Erich Mühsam's arrest. The poet Klabund wants to help his friend, get him released and stand with him. In the depths of the war he had written a passionate open letter to the German Kaiser appealing for peace, which had been published in the Swiss newspapers. And Klabund, who in the first months of war had been an ardent fighting patriot, had become a hero to Europe's pacifists. But he was also sick and needed mountain air. His wife Irene, to whom he had written endless paeans and whom he loved more than anything, had passed away shortly after the birth of his little daughter, and her death had thrown him completely out of kilter.

This nervous, gentle writer has barely set foot in Bavaria when he is taken into protective custody. No one really knows why—he certainly doesn't. He hasn't even begun to fight, to write, to free his friend Erich Mühsam.

The cold, dark, damp prison is torture for the consumptive poet. The loud, ruthless guards, the constant noise, the cold. He starts to write a diary at once. On Easter Sunday night he dreams of Irene again. "She was sitting in her silk wedding dress in the corner of a teashop, embroidering a child's shirt. It is six o'clock in the morning. The warden: 'Wake up! We can't wait for you! Take your lavatory bucket and empty it outside!' Sometimes I would like to stand up to them, but I can see it is wholly pointless. I am not exactly someone who commands respect. I look neither wild nor romantic, and who would be afraid of me? Not even the most timid child. I have a boy's face and they take me for an impulsive schoolboy who has joined in with the Spartacist ructions for a lark."

But he hasn't joined in with anything yet. Not even for a lark. He is a prisoner of the age. Turmoil in the world outside, and Klabund here in this cold cocoon. "The days go by. Time passes. Space crumbles. And nothing happens for me. Everything: in itself and for itself. I am quite outside the earth. In hell, I rotate around myself."

Nothing seems to be happening in Munich, either. Tense expectation. Sun. Spring holidays. A holiday from history. Victor Klemperer says of Munich on Easter Monday: "And sedately, delighted with this renewed world, already entirely accustomed to its strange novelty, the bourgeoisie goes for a stroll."

Then, on Tuesday, it's parade day. A show of strength from Munich's little Red Army. There are 15,000 participants in all. It passes off in a calm and civilized manner. The citizens watch. Some of them wave. But the calm is deceptive. Many people have begun to harbour a growing hatred. Hatred of all the disorder and uncertainty. Hatred of the brazen new rulers, many of whom come from Russia; hatred of the Jews, of all these "foreign elements" in power. For a while, it was an interesting curiosity. But how much longer is it going to go on? Hoffmann's government sends flyers raining down over the city on a regular basis. Telling the population to hold on. Salvation is on its way. Their liberators are already at the city gates.

An observer named Josef Karl has slipped inside the Wittelsbach palace on the day of the parade. To have a look around. To find his loathing confirmed. "The conditions there beggar all description," he writes. "A real Russian-Galician pigsty, the rugs and the floor dirty, as if they have not been scrubbed and cleaned for weeks. The rooms and hallways have entirely lost their former cleanliness and order, too. In every room being used as an office by the various councils there are a dozen Jews with their girl typists, the latter with their typical Russian hairstyles, cropped hair, voluptuous figures with low necklines and their 'ankle-length' skirts cut as short as possible, transparent silk stockings and ten- to fifteen-centimetre heels on their shoes." He summarizes: "Yes, these are the people who are shamelessly selling off and sucking dry the poor state of Bavaria." He himself, Josef Karl, the Bavarian, feels like a stranger in his own palace. "Every 'stranger' who does not belong in this house is regarded with fear and mistrust and measured up with suspicious eyes. Jewish foreigners with a real criminal aspect are the only ones at home here now. And we are already seeing the results of this Jewish economy."

A general irritation spreads—eventually infecting the rulers, too. Even Toller has started talking about "foreigners" who have snatched the reins of power. Recalling this period, he writes: "A few Russians win decisive political influence, for the sole reason that their passports identify them as Soviet citizens. The great feat of the Russian Revolution lends these men a magical lustre; experienced German communists stare at them as if dazzled. Because Lenin is a Russian, they assume these people share his abilities. The phrase 'In Russia we did it differently' overturns every decision."

Toller slowly sees his ideas, his idealism, his dreams vanishing. They are, after all, in the middle of a civil war. Nothing good, new, reconciliatory will come out of it.

Might they at least rescue the idea from this reality? Toller wants to negotiate with the Bamberg government. Leviné forbids it. He too knows that defeat is inevitable. But he wants a grand, bloody defeat. He is hoping it will generate fresh revolutionary energy for the future. At least, this is the motive Toller suspects.

Ernst Niekisch does in fact hasten to Bamberg for negotiations. But there is no point now. The Freikorps are on their way. The so-called White Guard, the White Army, named after the troops that fought the Bolsheviks, the Reds in the Russian Civil War. They are close to Munich, close to victory. No one can stop them now. They want capitulation. Berlin, too, wants capitulation. The Red carnival needs to be halted once and for all.

Toller just wants to prevent further bloodshed. On an almost daily basis he steps down from a position, is re-elected, goes out into the field, comes back to factory-council meetings. The workers still love him and believe what he says. He doesn't want their belief. All he can do is lie. Is he supposed to tell them all is lost? That it has all been for nothing? He can't do it. But nor does he want to be responsible for what will happen next. He wants to live, live, live. He knows he will die as soon as defeat comes. When the murdering begins in earnest.

The city is ruled by uncertainty and fear. On 26th April even Josef Hofmiller, who over all these weeks has greeted events in Munich with nothing but contempt and bile, recognizes that the mood has changed: "Something new is noticeable on the streets: a general mistrust of everyone by everyone." The city is buzzing with rumours of atrocities perpetrated by the White troops outside the city.

But rumours are circulating out in the countryside, too, in Bamberg and among the soldiers in their encampments. Out there, they hear all about the hundreds of murders supposedly committed in the city. The false claims and the fear take on a life of their own in these eddying days. No one knows anything, so they believe everything. There is no reliable source of news. There is fear, resentment, prejudice and hatred.

Who is for me? Who is against me? Even that much is no longer clear. There are hundreds of spies in the city. False communists. Comrades who might point a pistol at your back at any moment. The fact that everyone is armed does not help matters.

The central cell of resistance against the communist Council Republic is based in the lavish Vier Jahreszeiten Hotel. For months now the founder of the Thule Society, Rudolf von Sebottendorf, has been renting several rooms there. His organization, which grew out of a secret society called the Germanenorden, is based here, but almost all the other nationalist groups of these days, including the All-German Alliance and the German Workers' Party (DAP), founded by the Thule activist and sports journalist Karl Harrer in January 1919, also come together in the Vier Jahreszeiten. The editorial office of Thule's paper, the *Münchener Beobachter*, is also located there. The Oberland Freikorps was formed in these rooms. The DAP will later rename itself the NSDAP—the National Socialist German Workers' Party—and the *Münchener Beobachter* will soon become the *Völkischer Beobachter*, the official Nazi newspaper.

The Thule Society has no interest in re-establishing the monarchy. Their goal is to create a German dictatorship and drive all the Jews out of Germany. Their mottos are: "Keep your blood pure", and "Remember you are a German". The greeting the Thule members use among themselves is "*Heil und Sieg*", and their emblem a swastika surrounded by a starburst, behind an unsheathed sword. Their members are overwhelmingly academics, aristocrats and businesspeople.

The founder of this political secret society, Rudolf von Sebottendorf, was born Rudolf Glauer on 9th November 1875, the son of a locomotive driver in Hoyerswerda. He went to sea as a stoker before settling in Turkey in 1901. In Bursa he made the acquaintance of a Greek Jew, who introduced him to a Freemasons' lodge. Glauer developed a fervent interest in Sufism—Islamic mysticism. He wrote a book containing an admiring description of old Turkish Freemasonry and Rosicrucian traditions. Glauer became one of the first neo-Sufis in the West.

He claimed that in 1910 he founded a mystical lodge in Istanbul and was adopted by Baron Heinrich von Sebottendorf, who had also settled there. From then on, he called himself Rudolf von Sebottendorf. But no adoption certificate was ever found, and in 1919 the district authority in Freiburg declared that Glauer was not entitled to use the name, or the aristocratic "von".

In Turkey, he had taken Turkish citizenship and fought with the Ottoman Army in the Second Balkan War of 1913. After that, he returned to Germany and, as a Turkish citizen, was not called up for military service during the First World War. In 1915 he married Bertha Anna Iffland, the daughter of a rich Berlin businessman, and was then able to live off his wife's fortune. From which he took considerable sums to fund the propaganda activities of the Germanenorden and then the Thule Society.

Even during the war, the Germanenorden became known for its rabidly anti-Semitic propaganda. The members believed in the global Jewish conspiracy, and that conspiratorial means were required to put a stop to its game. This belief was constitutive for them. There was no question of the young Count Arco remaining a member once it became known that he had a Jewish mother. They might as well have shut up shop at once. Deeply ashamed, the young count had then chosen a particularly despised Jewish victim, to cleanse himself of the public humiliation. He wanted to become a German Thule hero, in spite of it all.

Now, in these April days, the anti-Semitic conspirators were at the height of their power. In total, the order had 2,500 members; the inner circle numbered 250. People were constantly coming and going from the rooms in the Vier Jahreszeiten, via a side entrance in Marstallstraße. The official head of the society, Friedrich Knauf, was a railway inspector and had procured papers that allowed spies and messengers to travel from Munich to Bamberg and back whenever they liked in the guise of railway officials. They had also obtained or forged all the official council government stamps.

In these days it was all too easy to betray the teetering republic. You didn't even need to forge stamps. One Thule member reported simply joining the Communist Party and being introduced to the wife of Fritz Seidel, the commandant of the military base in the Luitpold School.

This man immediately befriended Frau Seidel, and said that being accepted into the party had no value at all if he wasn't allowed to work for it. And so two days later he found himself doing some paperwork in the commandant's apartment in Müllerstraße. In the afternoon he was taken "in an elegant military car", as he put it, to the Communist Party's head office at the Leohaus in Pestalozzistraße. From the Vier Jahreszeiten to the Leohaus in just two days. He was put in charge of the office administration, which included the admission of new members to the Communist Party. Two triumphs in one: he could now admit whomever he liked to the party—especially those Thule members he trusted—and pocket the lists of real members. For the time to come. The time of revenge.

But apparently there are also lists of Thule members in existence, which now fall into the hands of the military police. And apparently, they were previously in the possession of Rudolf von Sebottendorf. Is he a traitor? Or simply incautious?

On 26th April the military police burst into the rooms of the Vier Jahreszeiten, arrest several members of the Thule Society and take them to the Luitpold School in Müllerstraße, which is being used as a barracks. Over the days that follow more prisoners arrive, including a few White Guard soldiers.

Then comes the 30th of April. It's over. The Council Republic is finished. A comrade brings Ernst Toller a passport and tells him to flee. He tears it up. It may be over, but his work is not yet done. To the very end, he still hopes he can prevent a bloodbath. He sets off for the War Ministry once more. He thinks: "We have failed. We have all made mistakes, we are all to blame, we have all fallen short—communists just as much as independents. Our venture has been in vain, our sacrifices all for nothing; but the workers trusted us. How can we justify ourselves to them now?"

He wants to go back to Dachau. Rudolf Egelhofer, the head of the Red Army, is sitting in the War Minister's office, looking crestfallen. Soldiers come and go, bringing one piece of bad news after another.

"Augsburg taken by the Whites."

"The Red troops are dispersing."

"Militias are springing up everywhere."

"In the villages, Red Guards are being disarmed, beaten and shot dead by peasants."

Egelhofer receives each message without a word. Gives Toller a pass for Dachau. Toller is back out on the street when he sees Egelhofer standing at the window, waving and shouting: "Toller! Toller!" He turns back. The head of the Red Army tells him he has just had a phone call. No one is going to get through to Dachau now. All the Red Army outposts have crumbled. There's no point any more.

Then a soldier rushes into the room. "The Whites have seized the central station!" he shouts. Within seconds, the War Ministry is empty. Toller, Egelhofer and his twenty-year-old adjutant are the only ones left. Egelhofer puts on his cap, shoves a revolver into his pocket, picks up two hand grenades. What is he planning to do, Toller asks. "I'm going to stay here," says Egelhofer. The young adjutant whispers: "I shall stay with you, Rudolf."

Then the phone rings. The information was false. The Whites aren't in the city yet. The end has not yet come.

———

On the night of 29th April, new prisoners were still being brought to the Luitpold School. There are now twenty-one men and one woman up on the second floor, in room forty-nine. The incarcerated White Guards are made to sweep the floor and wash bowls, as soldiers punch and kick them. Then, at ten in the morning, all the prisoners from room forty-nine are led out into the yard. There they learn that two of the three White Guards will now be shot. The two men are stood with their faces to the wall and left there for a few minutes, in mortal fear. Then they are ordered to turn around. The soldiers in charge tell jokes. Then they instruct the two to face the wall again and shoot them.

Afterwards, the other prisoners are taken into the school gym to peel potatoes for the Red Army. At half past twelve they go back to their room, where they are given "the lunch rations, which were good and plentiful," as the prisoner Wolfgang Kerschensteiner, the son of Munich's Director of Schools, later recalls.

At two o'clock a sentry comes into the room, takes the names of those present and with a disdainful look on his face explains that all prisoners are to be interrogated today. Another guard collects the first four for interrogation. A few minutes later, up in their room, the prisoners hear a commotion down in the yard, then a short address, then two salvos. Surely the interrogation can't be over yet, thinks Kerschensteiner—and, defying the guard's orders, he rushes to the window that overlooks the yard. There are the people who have just been led away, lying dead against the wall.

Very soon the next batch of prisoners is taken, including Prince Gustav von Thurn und Taxis, Hella, Countess von Westarp, who worked as a secretary to the Thule Society, and a Professor Ernst Berger, who has only just been brought in and who, as he has already admitted, has torn a rabble-rousing poster off a public wall. He goes with the others. A few minutes later, he's dead. Later it will be said that this was a misunderstanding. They hadn't meant to take the professor away.

Prince von Thurn und Taxis, however, manages to persuade them to bring him back upstairs. He says he was arrested under the name of Prince Albrecht, but that's not who he is. He asks them to check again. They bring him back up and compare the names on the list. But everything is in order: Prince Gustav von Thurn und Taxis is right there in black and white. He is taken back to the yard and shot.

Another group of three prisoners is taken, put up against the wall and shot. Then no one else comes in: the soldiers and Fritz Seidel, the commandant, have left the school in a panic. They are now afraid for their own lives. And in their fear, they leave the prisoners behind. The soldier who selected the prisoners to be shot commits suicide the same evening.

Meanwhile, the city's factory councils are gathering in the Hofbräuhaus for the last time; Ernst Toller is with them. Their power is gone, the Red Army dissolving. As Ernst Toller says later, they are intending to call on the workers of Munich to lay down their arms and receive the Whites in silence. The revolution has been defeated.

Then a man rushes in, runs up to the podium, cries out that ten people have been shot at the Luitpold School, ten "citizens of Munich". The factory representatives and the workers in the hall get up from their seats without a word. They are horrified. At the deaths. But also because they have an inkling of what this will mean for them and their comrades in the days to come.

Toller runs into the Luitpold School. The building is almost empty, save for a few young lads and two former Russian prisoners. Toller advises them to get out as quickly as they can. He hears shouts coming from behind a door. Are there still prisoners here? Does anyone have a key? No one replies.

They break the door down, and the sound of weeping and screaming suddenly falls silent; "and there in the corners of the room six people are crouching or kneeling, afraid for their lives. When we explain that we have come to release them, not to shoot them, they can hardly believe their ears."

Toller asks a soldier to take him to the shed in the yard where the bodies are lying. He strikes a match and sees the ten corpses by its flickering light. Toller has only one thought: they need to get the bodies out of there. The sight of them will unleash an orgy of revenge by the Whites. They need to go, at least until the storm that is now brewing has passed. He hopes Professor Sauerbruch will help him, the famous surgeon who brought Eisner's murderer Count Arco back to life, and who is treating Toller's girlfriend, the actress Tilla Durieux. Toller races over to the surgical hospital, speaks to Sauerbruch, begs him to have the bodies collected at once. But Sauerbruch is not about to collect anyone or anything.

News of the "hostage murders", the brutal killing of innocent citizens, is doing the rounds. A professor! A countess! By the next morning, rumours of the supposedly horrific mutilation of their bodies are on the lips of everyone in this city. The city that for a few weeks was a city of dreamers.

The 1st of May. The Freikorps march into Schwabing in wide columns. The citizens open their windows, they cheer, they wave their hands, white cloths, white handkerchiefs, anything that is white and can be waved. The troops are greeted like victors returning home from war. It's as if the Great War was won after all. It doesn't matter that these men are Prussians,

Württembergers, unruly Freikorps, entering the city as the White Army. The main thing is that the nightmare is over. It finally looks, as the reporter Victor Klemperer wrote the previous day, "as though we will be liberated from this ludicrous and senseless Hell".

It is as if someone has put the city through a darkroom overnight and turned a negative into a positive. All the red armbands, all the red flags have vanished. No one wants to have been a Red fighter now, no one a believer in the Council Republic, in the realization of crazy dreams. All that has vanished, has evaporated into jubilation. The reporter Klemperer mistrusts himself, his eyes, his writing. This is a cheap cliché he is witnessing. But he is witnessing it all the same. And he writes it up: "Today it is a commonplace and utterly untruthful newspaper cliché to say that incoming conquerors are 'cheered as liberators by the rescued population'. But regarding the arrival of these troops in Munich on 1st May 1919, there is really no other way I can put it. Bavarian heavy cavalry rode in, and Württemberg dragoons with red and black pennants, and Epp's Freikorps men with the golden lion's head in a black diamond on their upper arms, and Prussians with the white death's head of the Potsdam hussars on their caps. And all of them were greeted with cheers and waving handkerchiefs, and they were given cigarettes and cigars. It turned into a proper festival in front of the university, where Prussian troops had been billeted for the moment. For the first and only time in my life—the glory lasted all of two days—I witnessed a joyous Bavarian-Prussian brotherhood."

Just a few hours previously, at eleven o'clock in the morning, Klemperer had observed a little incident right outside the window of his apartment in Ludwigstraße. He heard a burst of gunfire, a falling bicycle. "I ran to the window and saw a

Red Guard standing next to the bike, and an elderly gentle-man gripping him by the arm, and a young man who tore the cartridge-studded scarf from his neck; the gun lay next to the bike at the edge of the sidewalk. The guard broke free and ran away, stripping off his red armband as he ran. That was the start of the bourgeois counter-revolution." And he was the last man Klemperer saw wearing a red armband.

The White troops march further into the city, taking over its symbolic buildings, and at around twelve o'clock two white flags and one blue and white are hoisted above the royal Residence. They are followed by flags over the city hall, the university, the War Ministry and finally the Wittelsbach palace. On Marienplatz, people give speeches standing on the Marian column. No one can really hear anything; they don't really want to hear anything. They want to shout "Bravo!" and throw their hats in the air. It's May!

Then the crowd is called to the Field Marshals' Hall. The people's army is to receive weapons. There are guns for every-one. For as long as the supply lasts.

Many Spartacists flee to the cellar of the Mathäserbräu, where it all began on 7th November. The city is armed. Where have all the rifles come from? What next? Has everything been decided?

It is as if an incredible energy has been building up in the city over the past six months. An energy that is now being discharged. At first in jubilation, in welcoming the White soldiers, in relief that the uncertainty is over. But this relief is very short-lived. For there is another feeling that has built up over all those months: hatred.

The people want revenge. Revenge for the fear they have felt, for their money, for their lives. Revenge too for this still incomprehensible, all-encompassing defeat that Germany was

forced to admit in autumn 1918. All the victims, all the dead
in this heroic war that had pitted justice against injustice.
Germany against the world. This war in which only reports
of victory had been heard and read from the battlefields until
the very last, and which was then so comprehensively lost that
the victorious powers are still brooding over the conditions
for a diktat that will destroy Germany.

After so many privations and sacrifices, the people feel they
have been cheated of victory. Of the parades, the celebrations,
the triumph. Now they want to have their parade. Celebrate a
little. And then take revenge for the lost war and the humili-
ations of recent months. Death to those responsible for it all.
Death to the Reds. Death to the Jews. Death to the Russians.

Oskar Maria Graf walks the streets of Munich. He looks. He
cannot comprehend it. "A terrible epidemic of denunciation
set in. No one was safe any longer. Anyone who had an enemy
could deliver him up to death with a few words. Now all at
once the bourgeoisie who had hidden away were back and
running busily after the troops, carrying rifles and wearing
blue-and-white armbands. Their eyes searched around with
true greed, they pointed this way and that, ran after someone
and struck him, shouting, spitting, lashing out like savages
before dragging the man, battered half to death, to the soldiers.
Or the process was even more rapid: the unsuspecting person
froze, the mob rushed up and surrounded him, a shot rang out,
and it was over. Everyone dispersed, laughing and satisfied."

He walks on towards Schwabing. Taking detours, always
sticking close to the walls of the houses. His friends Schorsch
and Ado have already been arrested. The artists' studios in
Schwabing were the first to be searched. Schwabing painters—
suspicious, the lot of them. One was shot dead on the street.

Graf wants to press on towards Dachau. An old woman is hobbling along the road. At the corner, a government soldier takes aim, there is a bang, the woman twitches a few times and then lies still. A girl cries: "God in heaven!" The bystanders all yell out: "Don't shoot! Don't shoot!" Then a boy wriggles out of the crowd and runs towards the body holding a fluttering red cloth. A bang. A shrill scream from the boy. He tumbles head over heels, then lies still. "These people are not human," Graf hears an old man say.

Everywhere, long lines of those who have been arrested move through the streets, beaten bloody, their hands in the air. Anyone who lowers an arm gets a rifle butt jammed into his back. Then the soldiers set about the trembling person with their fists.

Graf almost breaks down. "I wanted to cry out, but I just gritted my teeth and swallowed. There were tears pricking my eyes." He manages to pull himself together. He looks a prisoner in the eye.

"They are all my brothers, I thought contritely, they were brought into the world, beaten as children, thrown out, sent to a master where the beatings continued, exploited as journeymen, and finally they became soldiers and fought for the people who beat them.

And now?

They were all dogs like me. They'd had to cower and obey all their lives, and now, for wanting to bite, they were struck dead.

We are prisoners, all!—"

Graf goes the long way round back to Ludwigstraße. There hasn't been any shooting there for some time. The cafés on the garden squares have opened, and elegant folk are chatting and bustling about. "Bons viveurs with monocles were talking earnestly to soldiers and officers, while fine ladies dispensed cigarettes, cigars and chocolate, and flirted and joked with the mustachioed lieutenants."

The only thing Graf is waiting for now is his arrest. He longs for it. "I finally knew where and to whom I belonged."

The fronts are clear. There is only friend or foe. Freikorps soldiers will also write books about their experiences in these days. Manfred von Killinger, later a Nazi member of the Reichstag, calls his: *Serious and Humorous Incidents from Putsch Life.*

He writes that he went to the Luitpold School. He writes that he saw the corpses there. Everything that happened after that was completely and utterly justified by what he had seen there. And a lot is still to happen. All the floodgates are open.

"Anyone who sees this awful sight and still feels even a spark of sympathy for the killers deserves to suffer the same fate. War is violence, civil war is violence of the most potent kind. Moderation is stupidity—no, it is a crime against one's own people and country," says Killinger. And he goes on: "We know what will happen if these vermin are allowed to take the helm, they will cut our throats and smash our skulls in, like they did to the hostages in Munich. Very well! We promise to treat you in just the same way, and will smash your skulls in too, if you try to hinder us as we liberate the people."

Killinger is full of confidence. The struggles will end well for him and his comrades: "We will pave the streets with the heads of these people once again."

But at this point, many of the fantasists still have their heads. Ret Marut, the invisible Chief Censor and editor of the *Ziegelbrenner,* is trying to get to a meeting of "revolutionary and free-thinking writers" from across Germany. Ret Marut has not been fully informed of the day's events. He takes a seat in Café Maria Theresa in Augustenstraße, hoping to see some of the writers' conference delegates there.

But what he sees are White Guards shooting randomly into the crowd; before long he can see seven citizens lying in their own blood, two of whom die there on the street. A few paces away from the café a well-dressed man has been badly wounded. Marut and a few others try to get the wounded man off the street, where shots are still being fired, and into the café.

Then a truck comes speeding by, full of students with white armbands. When they see Marut, they stop. Although he has always stayed out of sight, they seem to know that he was a member of the Central Council. They seize him, search him for weapons. Marut—the editor of the pacifist *Ziegelbrenner*. He can't believe it. "You can, of course, search for truffles on a bare brick floor," he will later write.

They take him away and put him up before a military tribunal, which consists of "one dashing lieutenant" who quickly decides whether the accused is to be immediately shot or released, based on witness statements from those who have denounced him.

A few people are waiting in line before this one-man court-martial, with two soldiers standing guard. But the queue moves quickly, and soon there are only two: Marut and a mercenary. The mercenary fights back, complains, struggles and curses. And Marut manages to flee. He writes: "Two soldiers, in whom for a moment a spark of humanity may have flared as they saw what was being done with the most precious thing a person has—his life—were not uninvolved in this escape."

After that, the invisible Ret Marut disappears from Munich. No one sees him again. As the equally invisible B. Traven, he later settles in Mexico and writes adventure novels that become global bestsellers. When he is an old man, he will say of his former self: "Ret Marut was a political charlatan."

A man who was lucky to get away. Who vanished into thin air a few minutes before quite probably being sentenced to death.

Another man is walking down Königinstraße when he is arrested. The evidence against him: his long hair. It is Gustav Regler, who was once so enchanted by Eisner. Driven forward by rifle butts, he stumbles along to the next corner, where a collection of other prisoners is already waiting. They suspect they are going to be shot. It won't be long now. Then someone whispers in Regler's ear: "Let's make a run for it!" And, more urgently: "Get ready! I'm going to fling myself between the rifles!" At that moment a car roars towards them. Is there a drunk at the wheel? The car careers onto the pavement, knocking down one guard, then a second. The last soldier throws his rifle into the gutter and disappears.

Is he safe now? Gustav Regler is standing at the edge of the English Garden. "Spring," he thinks. "Oh God, it's spring!" Flowers in the grass, primroses, forget-me-nots, fresh, shining green leaves on the trees. Silence. A light breeze. Then a man in civilian clothes with a white armband steps out of the bushes. He asks Gustav Regler to move along: "This is where they're being shot," he says amiably.

He looks past the man to the little Monopteros temple. You can't see the firing squad. But you can see a man drop to the ground. Then the next volley and the next man falling. "I saw the men with their backs to the temple fall down like toy soldiers beneath its Greek columns," writes Regler.

Then the friendly man speaks up again from the bushes: "Here's a new lot coming." Twenty men in civilian dress, a chimney sweep in his work clothes with them. Led by two men from Württemberg in steel helmets. Regler steps onto the grass, for a moment feeling the temptation to join the troop. "I remember it well, it was like a feeling of pleasure." Then he recognizes Strasser among the prisoners, the theatre consultant and secretary of his student association. A few weeks ago he had wanted to take over the state theatre. "To revolutionize it from top to bottom," he had said. Regler thinks: "Because he had wanted to open the doors of the university to the sons of workers, he was now to be shot to ribbons by those same workers—worse still, by the very sons."

Regler hardly dares look at Strasser. The desire to join the death march has long since passed. Then out of the corner of his eye he sees Strasser making "the most moving gesture he could have made. His eyes met mine for an instant, then he looked quickly away, putting a finger to his lips. Watch out, beware of the enemy—that was what it meant. Watch out, don't betray anything! Whom might I betray? What might I betray? It was folly; it was paradox; and yet it was sublime, Roman, saintly in its nobility.

I at once put on a bored expression, to let him know I had understood. He should have his 'good exit'—wasn't that what they said in the theatre? I even went so far as to yawn and cover my mouth with my hand. Then I turned around and went slowly back towards the town.

I walked with ears strained, waiting for the volley that would end Strasser's life. But whether because the wind was the other way, or on account of some delay in the progress of the execution, I heard no other volley. I walked and walked, but there was only the sound of birdsong in the air. It was spring."

And what happens to the thin, bearded preacher? The original dreamer, the realizer of ideas who had wanted to reshape the world according to the hymns of Hölderlin and Walt Whitman, who had celebrated life's colour, had wanted to bring cosmic love and heartfelt emotion into the world, into children's schoolbooks, using Whitman's poetry, who knew that a revolution can only achieve its goal if it succeeds in reaching the children, revolutionizing the schools and universities, remodelling them and changing their militaristic and nationalist philosophy into a new, social thought that would bridge national divides. The man who strode so proudly through the palace crying out, "Here comes Landauer!" in the few days when he really had been permitted to shape things.

Even in recent days, he hasn't wanted to accept that it would remain a dream. Again and again he has tried to insinuate himself with the new powers. To bring them round to his way of thinking. But no one is interested in his contribution any longer. He was, after all, the Head Dreamer. Not the man for the hard fights that now have to be fought. And he had criticized dogmatic Marxism very sharply in his book *For Socialism*. His appeal for socialism concludes: "What does life matter? We will die soon, we all die. We do not live at all. Nothing lives but what we make of ourselves, what we do with ourselves. Creation lives; not the creature, only the creator. Nothing lives but the action of honest hands and the governance of a pure, genuine spirit."

They come in the early morning of 2nd May. He is staying with Kurt Eisner's widow. She has taken him into her apartment in the Großhadern district of Munich; his two daughters and the Eisner children are staying with relatives in Krumbach. Had he thought they wouldn't come for him? Did he believe they would think him innocent? After all, what has he done? He was the Education and Culture Minister in the government before last, the Culture Minister of Bavaria for six days, in which he tried to reform the schools and universities. Why should they arrest him? But Landauer already knows his fate. "Now death is on its way—one has to hold one's head high," he says.

They take him to Stadelheim. The moment he enters the prison yard the soldiers grow restive, some shouting that he should be beaten to death or shot. A lieutenant calms them down. For the moment, they mutter and leave Landauer in peace: he is to be taken into the jail's new building along with the other prisoners. There, someone hears Landauer murmur something about "piggish militarism". He immediately gets a punch in the face. More and more soldiers run after him. They are almost at the door when an officer, coming from behind them, shouts: "Halt! Landauer is to be shot at once!"

At almost the same time Baron von Gagern, a landowner and former major, arrives. He had fought in the battle for Munich as the leader of a voluntary patrol. He asks Landauer who he is. When he tells him, the baron strikes him in the face with his whip. That's the signal. That's what they have all been waiting for. A soldier called Eugen Digele, who knocked Landauer's hat off his head as soon as he set foot in the prison yard, also sets about him with a whip. Others use their fists. Landauer is said to have cried out: "Go on, beat me to death! And you call yourselves humans?"

A man comes in—not a single one of the hundred or so soldiers present will later admit they saw who it was. He has a rifle at the ready, he shouts: "I'll shoot him dead!"—and he fires at Gustav Landauer, hitting him in the left temple at point-blank range. Landauer falls. But is he still alive? Digele takes out his pistol and fires another shot into the right side of Landauer's head. A sergeant removes the dead man's coat. He remains lying face-down. But did he just move? A third bullet hits him in the back. An unknown soldier takes the watch and chain from the corpse, another tries to pull the ring off his finger. Other soldiers stop him. Digele takes the watch.

Eugen Digele is later sentenced to five weeks in prison for grievous bodily harm and receiving stolen goods. Baron von Gagern is given a fine of 500 marks. It is not possible to investigate any other perpetrators.

But the violence is far from over. One day later, Rudolf Egelhofer is shot without trial in the Munich Residence, where he was being held. On 4th May, a Lieutenant Pölzing receives an order from a Major Schulz to go to Perlach and arrest twelve workers whose names are on a list. He inquires with Hell, the local priest, who confirms that the wanted men are "agitators". The workers are captured without resistance and shot the next day without trial in the cellar of the Hofbräuhaus.

Two days later, on the evening of 6th May, in a Catholic club house on Karolinenplatz, twenty-three members of the St Joseph's Catholic journeymen's association are holding one of their weekly meetings, drinking beer and discussing a planned theatre performance, when a group of Prussian soldiers enters the room with bayonets mounted. They shout: "Hands up!" The surprised young men obey orders and, with a degree of violence from the soldiers, are taken out of the room, into the street and across to the Prince Georg Palace, where they are herded down into the cellar with rifle butts.

Why? Why? What is going on? "Shut your mouths!" the soldiers scream. Finally the young men learn that someone has denounced them as members of a Spartacist association. Red conspirators. The men insist they are from good families. They oppose the Spartacists. This is a misunderstanding. A survivor recalls: "Then came an agonizing sight that almost robbed me of my senses. One after another, people were shot dead without any hearing. When my friend declared he was a soldier himself, he was taken to one side. Now it was my turn to be shot. When my name was called—the rifle was already being aimed at me—one of the soldiers cried out: 'Stop! Don't shoot that one, I know him, he's the son of the palace cook!' It worked. The two of us who were left alive fled from this horror out into the night and ran to the caretaker's house, where we were given shelter. The soldiers sent a volley of twenty shots after us, though luckily none hit their mark. We broke down in a state of extreme agitation."

All the dead of these days are taken to Munich's eastern cemetery, the Ostfriedhof. Once he feels a little safer, Gustav Regler makes his way there. He has heard no more shooting since Strasser walked by him with his conspiratorial look in the English Garden. And now he wants to be sure. Is Strasser still alive? Or is he lying among all the others in the Ostfriedhof?

At the cemetery they have cleared out the greenhouses to make space for the bodies. Trucks are constantly bringing fresh corpses in. There are hundreds of them. Men stuff the bodies into crates laid ready for the purpose. Some are already full. Gustav Regler sees rivulets of red trickling out of them. A powerfully built man with a brown beard breaks the joints of bodies that don't fit into the crates. "It was a sharp sound at first, and then a pulpy one." The bearded man looks up, wipes the sweat from his forehead with the back of a bloodstained hand, and says to Regler: "If you're looking for someone, try over there on the left." Regler turns left down the rows of bodies. There he sees a grey *Litewka*, a double-breasted, tunic-like Prussian Army uniform jacket like the one Strasser had worn. "I walked until I came opposite the man in the jacket, and a great and bitter pain welled up in my heart. I raised a hand in greeting, as though it were a gesture of apology, and then bent down to look into Strasser's face.

Strasser no longer had a face. His shattered head seemed to make a mockery of any name by which one might call him." But Regler refuses to be mocked. He knows that Strasser lost two fingers of his right hand in the war. "I bent down and raised the right arm, to see if this was the man I was looking for.

But the arm also mocked me. It no longer had a hand.

I knelt staring at the stump that protruded from the sleeve, feeling dumb and helpless, like an animal that has been beaten too much. It was utterly devilish! I felt that too much was being asked of me."

Oskar Maria Graf has also come to view the dead. He, too, walks along the rows with others who are searching and mourning. "The dead workers lay on the dirty paving slabs. Thrown down, lying straight or crooked, on their backs or on their sides. It was only their feet that made a straight line against the wall. It smelled dreadfully of blood and corpses. We shuffled through the red-stained sawdust from one man to the next. Around me people whispered, wept, howled and whimpered, now and then bending down over the dead, to whom someone had attached parcel labels or little squares of pasteboard. There was a name or a number written on them." Oskar Maria Graf can hardly breathe. He wants to run away, but he is surrounded by people searching for their loved ones. He clenches his fists, he pulls himself together, he allows himself to be pushed onwards past the shattered bodies. He counts twenty, forty, seventy, ninety, a hundred and more. And then he stops counting. "I couldn't do it any longer. My eyes were streaming. I was freezing, trembling."

When he finally comes out, it's as if the whole city smells of corpses. He goes to the Dutchman's house in a kind of trance. "I drank, I talked, but I felt like it wasn't me at all." He counts in his sleep all night, he counts and counts and cannot see anything but that terrible mortuary.

In the villa on the Herzogpark, meanwhile, the mood is radiant. Thomas Mann begins his diary entry for the 1st of May with the proud announcement: "Erotic night." And he adds: "But one may not wish for calm *quand même*." On Easter Monday, his new son finally arrived. A forceps delivery; Katia suffered terribly. In the afternoon, the sculptor Schwegerle brought him an impressive bust of his head, for which he had spent a long time sitting. He took the bust upstairs at once to the exhausted Katia in her confinement room, placed it carefully on the pedestal where a bust of Luther had previously stood, and proudly presented—himself. "After a few experiments with the lighting it was shown to advantage and met with approval. It is very like."

On 1st May he is pleased to see the "good-looking" South German corps marching in, wearing their steel helmets. Everything is proceeding to his deepest satisfaction. Although that very morning he was called upon to write an article in favour of the Council Republic, and noted in his diary that he had found this request "not so rough", in other words, not entirely preposterous: "How can one avoid throwing in one's lot with communism, since it has the tremendous advantage of enmity towards the Entente? It has an air of mischief and cultural hottentotism about it, but in Germany it won't have that for long."

A day later this idea of an appeal on behalf of the Council Republic is long forgotten. The machinery is in motion. Order is moving in. "The Munich communist episode is over; there will be little desire to renew it. And I too cannot help but feel liberated and exhilarated. The pressure was despicable."

The next day, they get a visit. Soldiers ring the doorbell, introduce themselves as members of the new guard. They chat. They ask the Manns to telephone a Professor Marcks in case of any raids. They will then be informed at once. "I gave them cigars. The main station, said the spokesman, was in their hands, but the fighting would probably last for several more days. The Reds were 'all done for'; and if they fell into Red hands, their treatment would be just the same.—We gave a sentry some soup and a box of small fish."

Before supper, he talks everything through with Katia. Talks about Germany's new role in combatting Bolshevism, the "most terrible cultural catastrophe that has ever threatened the world". And "we spoke of the Russian Jew, the type who sits at the head of the global movement, this incendiary mix of Jewish intellectual radicalism and Slavic fanatical Christianity. A world with any instinct for self-preservation must take action against this breed of people, with all the energy and summary justice it can muster."

The following day he rejoices most of all in the fact that the newspapers finally start arriving again, and he can read about what has happened. "It will be pleasing to see what the journalists have to say about the base criminal economy that constituted the reality behind the 'idea'." Then the first edition of the *Münchner Neueste Nachrichten* finally arrives. It provides a chronology of events, focusing in particular on a wildly distorted account of the "hostage murders". This portrayal will only add more fuel to the bourgeoisie's hatred of the toppled government. Thomas Mann reads the paper aloud to Katia for more than an hour.

The day after next, 5th May, his friend Ernst Bertram comes to visit. Their disgust at the recent past is now so great that even France and the Entente are starting to look like the lesser evil. The two agree that "We have been peering into the abyss. The Entente is hateful, but the West has to be saved from the horrors of a mass migration from below."

That evening, Thomas Mann reads the evening paper. "A proclamation by the Möhl command calling for the elimination of the loutish type of soldier meets with my full approval. Incidentally, Löhr said that a good deal of neat 'cleaning up' by summary court-martial has been going on, which is certainly nothing to regret."

On 6th May Thomas Mann writes of the great-great-great-joy of the young Hans Castorp, who realizes how deeply rooted he is in his family tradition. And in the evening, Mann talks to his wife for the first time about the possibility of leaving Munich and moving to Lübeck, if things don't improve soon.

On 7th May his friend Emil Preetorius phones and asks if he is prepared to sign a statement warning "against arrogance and dangerous violence", to be published in the press. The statement says: "We believe it necessary, now in particular, for the bourgeoisie to turn its attention seriously and honestly towards the fact of its common fate with the working people. The fundamental transformation of the social order begins with them [...] It is useless to ask now who was the first to shed blood and feel horror in this struggle: the only important thing is who will find a way out of it and into a fruitful future for the whole nation." Thomas Mann signs, as do his brother Heinrich, Ricarda Huch, Rainer Maria Rilke, Bruno Walter and a few others.

A hopeless dream. So far removed from the reality out there. Clueless words. A well-intentioned gesture of friendship. But the gates of hell are open. The words of writers and poets will not close them again.

Out there, the murdering, hunting and denunciation continue. Many people are lucky to be in prison while Munich is thirsting for blood. Erich Mühsam, who has been an inmate of the Ebrach jail near Bamberg for several weeks now, suspects as much. His comrades say it in the prison yard, too: "Be glad you're in jail; in Munich you'd be dead." Mühsam, who so wanted to be Foreign Minister in the Council Republic, is of course even more reliant on rumours here in prison than the people out there. He hears that Toller and Landauer are dead, and he hears about the deaths in the Luitpold School and puzzles over who can have been behind them. He hears Levien is responsible, and if that is so, "I would be forced to believe that he is not right in the head." Sometimes there are newspapers. The Bamberg *Volksblatt* tells him: "The usual death by firing squad is much too good for the beasts of Munich, these bestial criminals should be hung in the public squares and put on display as a warning to brutish workers." Mühsam is also responsible for these appalling crimes, the paper says. No matter if he was already in jail when they were committed.

Mühsam notes: "They thirst for blood." He knows he isn't safe, even in prison. "Mühsam, make your peace with God," he urges himself. In his cell, he despairs. Hears about the horror. Can do nothing. "One looks around: nothing but bodies, nothing but murder victims—it is gruesome." His ideas, his ideals, his poems, his pamphlets. Everything Erich Mühsam lived and wrote for, all gone.

"That is the revolution that I ran jubilantly towards. A bloodbath after six months: I live in dread."

———

Adolf Hitler will later write in *Mein Kampf* that in the final days of the Council Republic he, too, was almost arrested and thrown in jail. By the Reds, naturally. "Three lads" tried to arrest him, Hitler writes, but he sent them fleeing with his "carbine raised".

There are no witnesses to this failed arrest. And no reason for it, either. He had, after all, just been elected deputy battalion representative. And he remained in that post until the Council Republic collapsed. Then, however, he was sure to have been one of the first to swap his red armband for a white one.

When his friend Ernst Schmidt sees him, he is extremely worried; Hitler looks "exhausted and quite ill". He tells Schmidt that the Whites forced their way into the barracks, took every man in Hitler's company prisoner, including him, and locked them in the basement of the Maximilian School. Then an officer who knew Adolf Hitler from the front intervened, and he was released.

He now really is caught between two stools. He held an official position in the Council Republic, and now he wants to be on the side of the new people in power. What to do? He volunteers as an informant for the investigation and discharge commission of the Second Infantry Regiment. Hitler is to report on the reliability of his own comrades during the Council Republic period. Or: denounce them. He immediately testifies against Josef Seihs, his predecessor as battalion representative, and against Georg Dufter, the former head of the demobilization company's battalion council. Men who until very recently held the same posts that he had. Dufter in particular, he said, had been an extremely dangerous rabble-rouser. "Dufter was the worst and most radical agitator in the regiment and was constantly engaged in propaganda for the Council Republic. In the regiment's public meetings he always took the most radical position and argued in favour of the dictatorship of the proletariat." Even on 7th May, Hitler says, Dufter encouraged "members of the regiment to join the Pioneers on this afternoon in hostilities against the government troops".

A man has switched sides in an instant and found his political home. There is no record of him having made a single anti-Semitic remark prior to these days—but in summer 1919 he is sent into the countryside for an army anti-Bolshevik propaganda course and instructed in the art of the propaganda speech. He will be highly praised by the course leader, although there is one area in which it seems necessary to curb this gifted thirty-year-old speaker. The course leader writes, diplomatically but clearly, that in his judgement: "Speeches which include an unambiguous discussion of the Jewish question with particular reference to the Germanic point of view might easily give Jews an opportunity to describe these lectures as anti-Semitic. I therefore thought it best to command that discussion of this topic should be carried out with the greatest possible care, and that clear mention of foreign races being detrimental to the German people is to be, if possible, avoided."

His student will not follow this friendly advice. A man has found his purpose in life. His talent. And his enemy.

But it is still spring. People are still being denounced, arrested and shot. Now it's Oskar Maria Graf's turn. It's the morning after the night he spent counting. He is almost relieved when they finally come for him. They lock him in a hopelessly overcrowded cell. He is greeted with a loud cry of: "So, you innocent too, then?" Everyone laughs.

At first he is glad not to be alone, but later he will suffer. It's so cramped that they have to sleep standing up. Or try to.

Someone complains that it's too full in there. "It'll be emptier soon," the guard calls in. "Yes, when another dozen men get shot!" the prisoners shout back. Men keep being taken away for interrogation. Some return. Others don't. Transferred to another prison? Shot?

A new arrival says that Eugen Leviné, or Leviné-Nissen as the prisoners here call him, has been captured. It is the 13th of May. Consternation in the mass cell. Where is he? In a cell on his own? Is it really true?

And suddenly some of them are shouting out: "Hurrah for Leviné-Nissen!" A more cautious man tries to silence them. "Don't say that, it'll be the worse for us." "Coward!" the others retort. And finally everyone shouts: "Hurrah for Leviné-Nissen!"

The men are seized by "an embittered boldness", as Graf calls it. They shout and sing. At first the "Marseillaise", though unfortunately most of them only know one verse. Then the "Internationale", splendid, everyone knows that. Graf teaches them the "Heckerlied", a song from the last German Revolution in 1848. No one knows it but Graf. He goes through the song with his fellow inmates line by line until they are all singing:

> When the people ask you,
> Is Hecker still alive?
> Why then sir you can tell 'em:
> Yes, he's still alive.
>
> He hangs not from a scaffold, sir,
> He hangs not from a tree.
> But still he hangs on to the dream
> Of a people's Germany

Princes' blood must flow now
Through the city streets
And from it there will flower
A republic of the free.

For more than thirty years now
Our serfdom has gone on
Down with all the devils
Of the reaction!

At some point the guards bring another new prisoner into the cell. A worker of around forty years old. He is distraught, enraged, shouting: "My wife is dying! My wife! Let me out!" The men try to calm him down, they reason with him, they hold him still. But he refuses to be calmed. He lashes out, throws himself to the floor. They dip a handkerchief in water from the toilet and lay it on his forehead. He weeps silently to himself.

Some time later the guard comes to the cell door. "Kastenberger!" he shouts callously, "Your wife has died!" Then he walks on. The prisoners expect another outburst. But there is nothing. The man crumples a little and crawls back onto his bench.

Later that night they hear dull thuds and a rattling, panting sound. Kastenberger is smashing his skull against the wall with all his might. When they try to overpower him, he nearly bites their fingers off. He is badly injured, covered in blood; he stops moving and doesn't reply when they talk to him. He is not taken away for another two days.

After his release, Oskar Maria Graf bumps into another man from the cell on the street. The man tells him about his father, who was shot dead in the Hofbräuhaus; about his wife, who suffered a premature birth. "She's not been right since," he says. And that he never wanted anything to do with this revolution. But they came for him anyway, dragged him out of bed on 1st May. The policemen beat him all the way to the prison. "There—there ain't no God," he says. Oh yes, and has Graf heard about Kastenberger? He started ranting and raving again in the transport, after they took him from the cell. So they killed him.

Wordlessly, Graf strokes his former cellmate's head. "It has not all been for nothing," he says, without conviction, half to himself, half to the other man.

The other man slowly calms down. They walk on. He makes a fist. He shouts: "If it starts again, I'm going to fight... I'll fight until they break me... then at least I'll know I did it for us." And he adds: "The hour is coming."

Graf trembles slightly and looks at his comrade, who squeezes Graf's hand before disappearing, silent and alone, into the darkness.

"I stood there, thinking, wanting to call out to him, go after him; and then I set off for home. My heart grew hotter and hotter. I saw again all the images that had burned themselves into my memory: the crowds in the streets, the army of workers, the dismal columns of prisoners, the bodies of those who had been shot, and this one comrade. And everything grew even sharper and even more inextinguishable. And this one man with his raised fist became legion. I let out a cry: 'The hour is coming!'

'It has not all been for nothing!' I repeated, wholeheartedly.

My tiny circle shattered. I was more than just 'I'. A great happiness flowed through me."

———

Naturally, the prisoners' shouts for Eugen Leviné had no effect at all. In June he is charged with high treason. He doesn't stand a chance. In his closing statement to the court, he says: "There you are: the Majority Socialists start all this and betray us, the Independents fall for it, join in, then capitulate, and we Communists are put up against the wall. We Communists are all dead men on holiday. Of that much I am aware. I don't know if they will extend my holiday or whether I must march off to join Karl Liebknecht and Rosa Luxemburg. In any case, I face your pronouncement with composure and with inner peace. For I know what it will mean. Events are not to be halted." At two o'clock on the afternoon of 5th June, Eugen Leviné is shot by order of a court-martial.

Six days later, Rainer Maria Rilke bundles up all his letters and packs them into a leather trunk. He stashes a collection of journals from the past few years, manuscript beginnings and other papers in the bureau, and gives the bureau key to Elya Maria Nevar, who is helping him pack. He takes a cab to the station and gets on a train to Switzerland. He will never return to Germany.

Twice the White troops have searched his apartment. He had accidentally left a notice from the council government pinned to the door, saying that this apartment was under the personal protection of the councils.

Later, in Switzerland, looking back at the period of the Council Republic, he writes: "Germany could have, in the moment of collapse, shamed and shaken everyone, the world, through an act of deep truthfulness and repentance. At that time I hoped for a moment..."

Now he no longer hopes for anything. Not from politics, not from the world. He has gone back to writing poetry—short

verses with dedications at first. This one is for a Fräulein
Hedwig Zapf:

> We turn our face to that which does not know us:
> to trees that rise and dreamfully exceed us,
> to all things self-replete, to every silence—
> yet through our very turn the circle closes,
> and via everything that is not ours
> brings back to us a brightness all along.
> O things, if you could stand among the stars!
> And nothing is disturbed as we live on...

Between poems, Rilke also writes a testimony for his far-off
friend Oskar Maria Graf. He is "as a man and as a writer, filled
with the purest and most humane intentions", he writes.
Regrets how infrequently he was able to speak to him. But
recalls Graf's one excursion into the world of political speaking, that time in December when he spent all the rich lady's
money on posters and the time it took to put them up, but
forgot his political demands. "Oskar Maria Graf's one attempt
to appeal to the masses betrayed how much the path of pure
fellow feeling corresponded to his ideals."

For his part, Rilke leaves behind a few more poems for
the writers of the political awakening. He leaves them to the
author Alfred Wolfenstein for his political, literary, emphatic
anthology The Uprising, which is published in these days. Too
late? Too early? At the right time? Rilke wants this poem to
speak for him:

> Exposed on the mountains of the heart. Look,
>   how small there,
> look: the last hamlet of words, and higher,

and smaller still, a last
farmstead of feeling. Can you see it?
Exposed on the mountains of the heart. Stony ground
beneath your hands. Still, something will
bloom here; from the silent precipice
an unknowing herb blossoms, singing.
But the knowing? Ah, you who began to know
are silent now, exposed on the mountains of the heart.
Many creatures with whole, conscious minds
may roam the slopes; assured mountain beasts
pass and linger. And that great bird
safely circles peaks of pure denial. But we
are not safe, here on the mountains of the heart.

A few weeks previously, Rainer Maria Rilke had visited Ernst Toller in one of his hiding places. The whole city, the whole country was covered in wanted posters bearing his photograph. "Ten-thousand-mark reward for high treason." "Toller is of slender build, between 1.65 and 1.68m tall, has a thin, pale face, no beard, large, brown, piercing eyes, closes his eyes when thinking, has dark, almost black wavy hair, speaks standard German."

Munich is looking for Toller. Ten thousand marks is a fantastic reward. Toller knows that if they find him, he's a dead man. It isn't all that long since a false Ernst Toller was shot. And another on 1st May. Someone else was beaten to death because he bore a distant resemblance to the wanted man. The police called in the chauffeur who had driven Toller to Dachau to identify the body; he recognized Toller in the Ostfriedhof morgue and sobbed bitterly. Toller's mother read the news in the paper. For three days she sat in mourning on a low footstool, draped cloths over all the mirrors. On the fourth day she learnt that her son was still alive.

Toller bleaches his hair to a shade of orange, grows a moustache, scurries from one hiding place to another. A female friend invites Rilke to visit. He brings Toller's friend a bunch of long-stemmed roses, and regrets that he cannot take Toller in because the authorities keep searching his apartment—he is terribly sorry. He says of Toller: "Dull grey eyes beneath heavy lids look sadly and warily at me, then his gaze and the tips of his drooping moustache fall towards his hands."

Finally Toller finds slightly more secure accommodation with the painter Hans Reichel in "Suresnes", a small stately home in Schwabing where Reichel has a studio apartment. Here Toller can even make brief forays into the garden from time to time; breathe. He reads in the papers that people are searching for him right across Germany, that trains are being stopped, villages encircled. They are even searching in Austria and Switzerland. A cousin of his is arrested, even though he is fighting with the Epp Freikorps and has sworn he will shoot Toller on sight without a second thought. Everyone is a suspect. The whole country is in the grip of Toller hysteria.

A house search in Römerstraße. Two detectives are turning over an apartment when the doorbell rings. One of them opens the door cautiously; there are soldiers outside. The leader shouts: "There's Toller!" One of the soldiers shoots and the detective falls to the floor, dead.

Eventually, after more than a month, it finally happens. As they are searching the apartment of the painter Johannes Reichel, they find the secret door in the wall behind which Toller is hiding. He opens it himself from inside. "You're looking for Toller. I am he."

He is arrested and led through the city. His city.

"We walk through the empty streets as dawn is breaking. Three soldiers march in front, and I follow, handcuffed to a policeman on either side; three soldiers with their rifles at the ready bring up the rear.

On Luitpoldstraße a clock strikes five. An old woman is hobbling along to Mass, and at the church door she turns and sees me.

'Have you got him?' she cries. Then she lowers her eyes and prays as the rosary slides through her fingers. And then, from the open church door, the wrinkled mouth screeches: 'Kill him!'"

Ernst Toller is lucky. Had he been discovered just a few days earlier, he would certainly have been shot. They place him in the death-row cell of his old adversary Eugen Leviné, just one day after the latter has left that cell on his final walk.

In court, Thomas Mann, Max Weber and others vouch for Ernst Toller. They vouch for his integrity. The sentence is five years' imprisonment in a fortress.

He has not long been in his new cell when he looks out of the window and sees "A young man with a bandaged, chubby, childlike face crossing the courtyard. 'That's Eisner's murderer, Count Arco,' says the warder. So this smiling boy is Eisner's murderer. This child's deed precipitated the attempt on Auer's life, the confusion that followed, the Council Republic, its downfall and the wrath of the Whites."

Count Arco will be released from prison before Ernst Toller. On his return home to his castle in St Martin im Innkreis, the village will hold a lively celebration. One newspaper reports that: "In the evening the people gathered in a lantern procession with music in front of the castle. Following this in the castle courtyard there was a convivial gathering, with several speeches given in praise of the heroic count. Late at night, the young Arco was led into the castle amid cheering, flag-waving and music."

Ernst Toller, too, becomes a star in prison. He writes plays that are performed to great acclaim across the country, and a collection of poems about the swallows that have made their nest in his cell. He places these lines at the start of the book:

> A friend died in the night.
> Alone.
> The prison bars kept watch.
> Autumn will come soon.
> The ache, the ache burns deep.
> Abandonment

He is released in July 1924. He stands at the window of a train compartment and looks out into the night. And writes:

> No, I was never alone in those five years, never alone in my comfortless abandonment. I took comfort in the sun and the moon, the wind that caressed the puddles and rippled vanishing circles into them, the grass that grew in spring between the stones in the yard, a good view, a greeting from someone I loved, the friendship of my comrades, my belief in a world of justice, freedom, humanity, a world without fear or hunger.
> I am thirty years old.
> My hair is turning grey.
> I am not tired.

BEACH

THE SEA. A long, wide beach of white sand. A pier stretches out into the ocean, a good 150 metres long, a path into the open that ends in nothingness. Large hotels line the promenade. A little further inland, an old, white house stands in the sand, shaded by trees. It was built by Carlos Gesell in the early 1930s, here in the dunes on the Argentinian sea, 400 kilometres south of Buenos Aires. His father, Silvio Gesell, had died shortly before, in 1930, in a vegetarian colony called Eden, in Oranienburg to the north of Berlin, where he had spent the final years of his life. He had lived in Argentina himself for a long time, and as a twenty-five-year-old in 1887 had opened a shop in Buenos Aires selling dental supplies. He wrote his first treatise on "decaying money as a means of stabilizing economic circulation" as early as 1891.

His son Carlos was a businessman and ran the family firm in Buenos Aires. Casa Gesell was famed for its children's furniture. Carlos had been to the Belgian seaside resort of Ostend not long before his father's death, and had been overwhelmed by the long beach, the glamour of the town, the sea. And then on a trip to southern Argentina he had discovered this gigantic stretch of dunes, which reminded him of the beach in Ostend—just without any houses or people. He bought the beach for next to nothing: who wants wind-blown sand in the middle of nowhere.

Carlos Gesell intended to plant pine trees there and use the wood for his children's furniture. But no pines would grow. Nothing grew there at all. Several times he flew to Europe and brought back seeds for plants that grow in dune sand: marram grass from Sylt, other beach grasses, pines, acacias. He sought advice from an agricultural engineer who had successfully planted the dunes of the East Frisian Islands. But to no avail. One storm was enough to blow away every last tender little plant.

Sometimes people came by and laughed. "The madman in the dunes," they called him. But then some big-game fishermen from Buenos Aires weighed anchor on Gesell's stretch of coast, raving about the tremendous wealth of fish to be had in the sea there. And Carlos Gesell thought that maybe he could attract visitors, tourists, anglers, beach-lovers to his dunes, and he built a road. He called it Bulevard Silvio Gesell, after his father. He built a little guest house, too: La Golondrina, "the swallow".

Today, 30,000 people live in the town that Carlos named Villa Silvio Gesell, which was later shortened to Villa Gesell. And trees now grow on the dunes. For many years it was a haven for hippies—artists, entertainers, writers, self-liberators—and today it's one of Argentina's most popular holiday resorts. Every year, 750,000 tourists visit a place named after the Finance Minister of the Munich Council Republic.

And in summer, when you see the crowds of happy holidaymakers strolling down the Bulevard Silvio Gesell, looking for ways to fritter away their money, you could almost take them for late disciples of the shrinking-money theorist, whose organic money was designed to lose value within a week: money should be transformed into use and pleasure, instead of languishing joylessly, pointlessly in bank accounts.

There were others, too, whose lives continued like the plot of a novel.

The founder of the Thule Society, who called himself Rudolf von Sebottendorf and had been thrown out of his own club following the hostage murders, lost his entire fortune speculating on the stock market. He founded an astrological magazine and later claimed that he had been honorary consul in Mexico between 1923 and 1928, though otherwise he lived mostly in Turkey. After the National Socialists took power he came back to Germany in high spirits and wrote a book entitled *Before Hitler Came*, in which he traced the roots of the Nazi Party back to his Thule Society, proving that it was actually he, Sebottendorf, who had come up with the whole idea. The book was banned, Sebottendorf was deported, and he returned to Istanbul. When news reached him of the German capitulation on 8th May 1945, he drowned himself in the Bosphorus.

In his later life Ernst Niekisch, the calm, circumspect voice of reason during Munich's revolutionary months, personally lived through the extremes of the century. After the council government was crushed, he left the SPD and joined the USPD, where he developed an increasing aversion to the internationalist aspect of Marx's doctrine and began to pursue a new, national socialism. He then joined the "Old Social Democratic Party" and started a magazine called *Widerstand*—resistance—to which the popular right-wing authors Ernst and Friedrich Georg Jünger also contributed. He developed a programme of "national rebirth for Germany", published pamphlets against "negro-ized France" and inflammatory anti-Semitic literature. "Wherever there is an economy, you will find the Jew at the top," he wrote. In 1932 Ernst Niekisch warned against Adolf Hitler, whom he thought "too legalistic", in the pamphlet *Hitler: A German Catastrophe*. In 1939 he was sentenced to life imprisonment for high treason by the fascist People's Court. In prison in Brandenburg, he went almost blind.

After the war he sneered: "When the Third Reich began to compete with world Jewry, it raised the latter back to the height of a world power." He joined the German Communist Party, and later the Socialist Unity Party (SED). In 1948 he was appointed Professor of Sociology at the Humboldt University in East Berlin, then became an MP in the first East German People's Parliament. After the uprising of 17th June 1953 he stepped down from all political offices, before leaving the SED in 1955 and moving to West Berlin in 1963, where he died four years later.

Sebastian Haffner called Ernst Niekisch the "last great Prussian" and "Hitler's adversary", and added in 1980: "The true theoretician of the global revolution that is currently in progress is not Marx, not even Lenin. It is Niekisch."

Everyone's novel came to an end. We know of many deaths. Erich Mühsam was brutally murdered in 1934 at a concentration camp in Oranienburg, though there was an amateurish attempt to make it look like a suicide. In his Second World War diaries, Ernst Jünger wrote that he thought the people who had just searched his house "were looking for letters from the old anarchist Erich Mühsam, who had developed a childish affection for me and who was murdered so horribly. He was one of the best, most good-natured people I have ever met."

The American Ben Hecht was lured to Hollywood in 1926

by a telegram from a friend: "Millions are to be grabbed out here and your only competition is idiots. Don't let this get around." And so he went. He made films with Ernst Lubitsch, Otto Ludwig Preminger and Alfred Hitchcock; his screenplays were nominated for an Oscar six times and won twice. From the start, he was outraged by the American public's indifference to the threat that Nazi Germany posed to the Jews, and placed adverts in New York newspapers designed to shake people awake. One of these "announced that 70,000 Jews of both sexes had been offered for sale by the Romanian government at fifty dollars a head. They were, our ad vouched, guaranteed human beings."

Oskar Maria Graf lived in exile in New York for many years. He said of himself: "In the bars groups of regulars, all of them Germans, always formed around me at once." He got a friend to make him a wooden sign for the table where his regular circle met, bearing the inscription: "We are in favour of everyone and everything."

Silvio Gesell defended himself before the court in Munich. "Hands off Silvio Gesell!" he cried out in his final plea. He was acquitted.

Several more experiments with his free money were carried out in various places around the world. One in Wörgl, Austria, in 1932, must have been unusually successful. For some time afterwards people talked about the "Wörgl miracle", and even the French Finance Minister and later Prime Minister Édouard Daladier visited to see for himself the miraculous power of this vanishing money. The American economist Irving Fisher suggested to the US government of the day that they should try to perform their own Wörgl miracle, with a scheme that went by the name "Stamp Scrip". The government did not embrace the idea.

In the early days, the National Socialists also made frequent reference to Gesell's theories in their economic drive to "end the slavery to interest".

The most significant economist of the twentieth century, John Maynard Keynes, wrote in detail about this "strange, unduly neglected prophet", and predicted "that the future will learn more from the spirit of Gesell than from that of Marx". And when Benoît Coeuré, a board member of the European Central Bank, gave a lecture to its Money Market Contact Group in spring 2014 on the apparently new phenomenon of negative interest, he explained to the bankers present that the idea of negative interest and the taxation of money went back to the financial theorist Silvio Gesell, who had once, for a few days, been the People's Delegate for Finance in the Munich Council Republic.

Ernst Toller made many speeches in his life. And each of them gave the impression that he was above all talking to himself. That he painstakingly had to build himself up to this great confidence that he always exuded, the confidence for which his audiences and readers loved him.

The "I am not tired" with which our story ends is also the last line of his autobiography. I have read the words so often. You sense that it might not be true. Here is a young man ending the novel of his life at the age of thirty. He has already suffered too many defeats. His hopes were too great, and they ended in the Luitpold School, the Ostfriedhof, outside Dachau. "I am not tired" is the reveille for a man who would really like to sleep. To rest. To watch the swallows. And who goes on fighting because he has to.

They were the first. They were entirely unprepared for it all, after 900 years of the Wittelsbach dynasty, after losing an unlosable war. There were no historical precedents for them to draw on. Direct, permanent democracy; everyone having a say in everything. A government of fantasy and fictions. They wanted the best and created horrors.

Officially, 606 deaths were registered following the suppression of the Council Republic: 233 Red Army soldiers, 335 civilians, 38 members of the Freikorps. Estimates suggest there were a further 400 deaths. In the weeks after the revolutionaries were defeated, 2,200 supporters of the Council Republic were court-martialled and sentenced to death or imprisonment.

In *I Was a German*, Toller wrote: "You cannot just avoid reality when it is different from what you wished it to be, and excuse yourself by saying: that was not what I intended."

But the lesson from all the defeats is certainly not to grow feeble, to give up, to sleep, not even to begin.

"We do not love politics for politics' sake," he said in June 1936 at a writers' congress in London. "We take part in political life today, but we believe it is not the least significant aspect of our battle to free future mankind from the wretched competition of interests that goes by the name of 'politics' today. We are ploughmen, and we don't know if we will be reapers. But we've learned that 'fate' is an excuse. *We* make fate! We want to be true, we want to be courageous, and we want to be human."

He went on giving his speeches in exile in New York, even on the evening of 21st May 1939. He spoke about his precursor Heinrich Heine, about Georg Herwegh, Ludwig Börne. And about the present, and the loud, unignorable voice of authors in exile: "This voice is so powerful that Hitler cannot drown it by the screams of his rage." The next day, he hanged himself in his room at the Mayflower Hotel.

He had believed in what was good to the point of madness. And despite all the futility he had been right. This story may have turned out badly. But it is far from over. Tiredness is not an option.

SELECT BIBLIOGRAPHY

Gesell, Silvio, *The Natural Economic Order*, tr. Philip Pye (London: Peter Owen, 1958)

Graf, Oskar Maria, *Prisoners All*, tr. Margaret M. Green (New York, NY: A.A. Knopf, 1928)

Hecht, Ben, *A Child of the Century* (New York, NY: Donald I. Fine, Inc. 1954)

Hesse, Hermann, *Demian: The Story of Emil Sinclair's Youth*, tr. W.J. Strachan (London: Picador, 1995)

Hesse, Hermann, *If the War Goes On… Reflections on War and Politics*, tr. Ralph Manheim (New York, NY: Farrar, Straus and Giroux, 1970)

Hofmiller, Josef, *Revolutionstagebuch 1918/19: Aus den Tagen der Münchner Revolution* (Leipzig: Karl Rauch Verlag, 1938)

Keynes, John Maynard, *The General Theory of Employment, Money and Interest* (London: Palgrave Macmillan, 1936)

Killinger, Manfred v., *Ernstes und Heiteres aus dem Putschleben* (Munich: München Zentralverlag der NSDAP, 1941)

Klemperer, Victor, *Munich 1919: Diary of a Revolution*, with a foreword by Christopher Clark and a historical essay by Wolfram Wette, tr. Jessica Spengler (Cambridge: Polity Press, 2017)

Kolb, Annette, "Mit Kurt Eisner und Hugo Haase in Bern", in: *Kleine Fanfare* (Berlin: Ernst Rowohlt Verlag, 1930)

Kuhn, Gabriel (ed.), *All Power to the Councils! A Documentary History of the German Revolution of 1918–1919* (Oakland, CA: PM Press, 2012)

Landauer, Gustav, *For Socialism*, tr. David J. Parent (Candor, NY: Telos Press, 1978)

Landauer, Gustav, *Revolution and Other Writings: A Political Reader*, ed. and tr. Gabriel Kuhn (Oakland, CA: Merlin Press, 2010)

Mann, Golo, *Erinnerungen und Gedanken: Eine Jugend in Deutschland* (Frankfurt am Main: S. Fischer Verlag, 1986)

Mann, Klaus, *The Turning Point: Autobiography of Klaus Mann* (London: Serpent's Tail, 1987)

Mann, Thomas, *Death in Venice and A Man and His Dog: A dual-language book*, ed. and tr. Stanley Applebaum (Mineola, NY: Dover Publications, 2001)

Mann, Thomas, *Diaries, 1918–1939*, tr. Richard and Clara Winston (New York, NY: Harry Abrams, 1982)

Mann, Thomas, *Letters of Thomas Mann, 1889–1955*, vol. 1, 1889–1942, tr. Richard and Clara Winston (London: Secker & Warburg, 1970)

Mann, Thomas, *Reflections of a Nonpolitical Man*, tr. Walter D. Morris (New York, NY: Frederick Ungar, 1983)

Mann, Thomas, "That Man is My Brother", *Esquire*, 1st March 1939, pp.131–3

Mann, Thomas, *The Magic Mountain*, tr. H.T. Lowe-Porter (London: Vintage, 1999)

Mitchell, Allan, *Revolution in Bavaria, 1918–1919: The Eisner Regime and the Soviet Republic* (Princeton, NJ: Princeton University Press, 1965)

Mühsam, Erich, *Liberating Society from the State and Other Writings: A Political Reader*, ed. and tr. Gabriel Kuhn (Oakland, CA: PM Press, 2011)

252

Regler, Gustav, *The Owl of Minerva: The Autobiography of Gustav Regler*, tr. Norman Denny (London: Rupert Hart-Davis, 1959)

Rilke, Rainer Maria, *Letters of Rainer Maria Rilke*, vol. 2, 1910–1926, tr. Jane Bannard Greene and M.D. Herter Norton (New York, NY: The Norton Library, 1972)

Rilke, Rainer Maria, *Poems 1906–1926*, tr. J.B. Leishman (London: The Hogarth Press, 1976)

Schmolz, Gerhard (ed.), *Revolution und Räterepublik in München 1918/19 in Augenzeugenberichten* (Munich: Deutscher Taschenbuchverlag, 1978)

Spengler, Oswald, *The Decline of the West: An Abridged Edition*, tr. Charles Francis Atkinson (New York, NY: A.A. Knopf, 1961)

Toller, Ernst, *I Was a German*, tr. Edward Crankshaw (London: John Lane, The Bodley Head, 1934)

Toller, Ernst, *Letters from Prison, Including Poems and a New Version of The Swallow Book*, tr. R. Ellis Roberts (London: John Lane, The Bodley Head, 1936)

Toller, Ernst, *Plays One*, tr. and ed. Alan Raphael Pearlman (London: Oberon Books, 2011)

Watt, Richard M., *The Kings Depart. The Tragedy of Germany: Versailles and the German Revolution* (London: Weidenfeld & Nicolson, 1969)

Weber, Thomas, *Becoming Hitler: The Making of a Nazi* (Oxford: Oxford University Press, 2017)